AF585103

Coney Island Malibu Beach

Benjamin Acree
Robert S. Johnson
Jackson Eaton

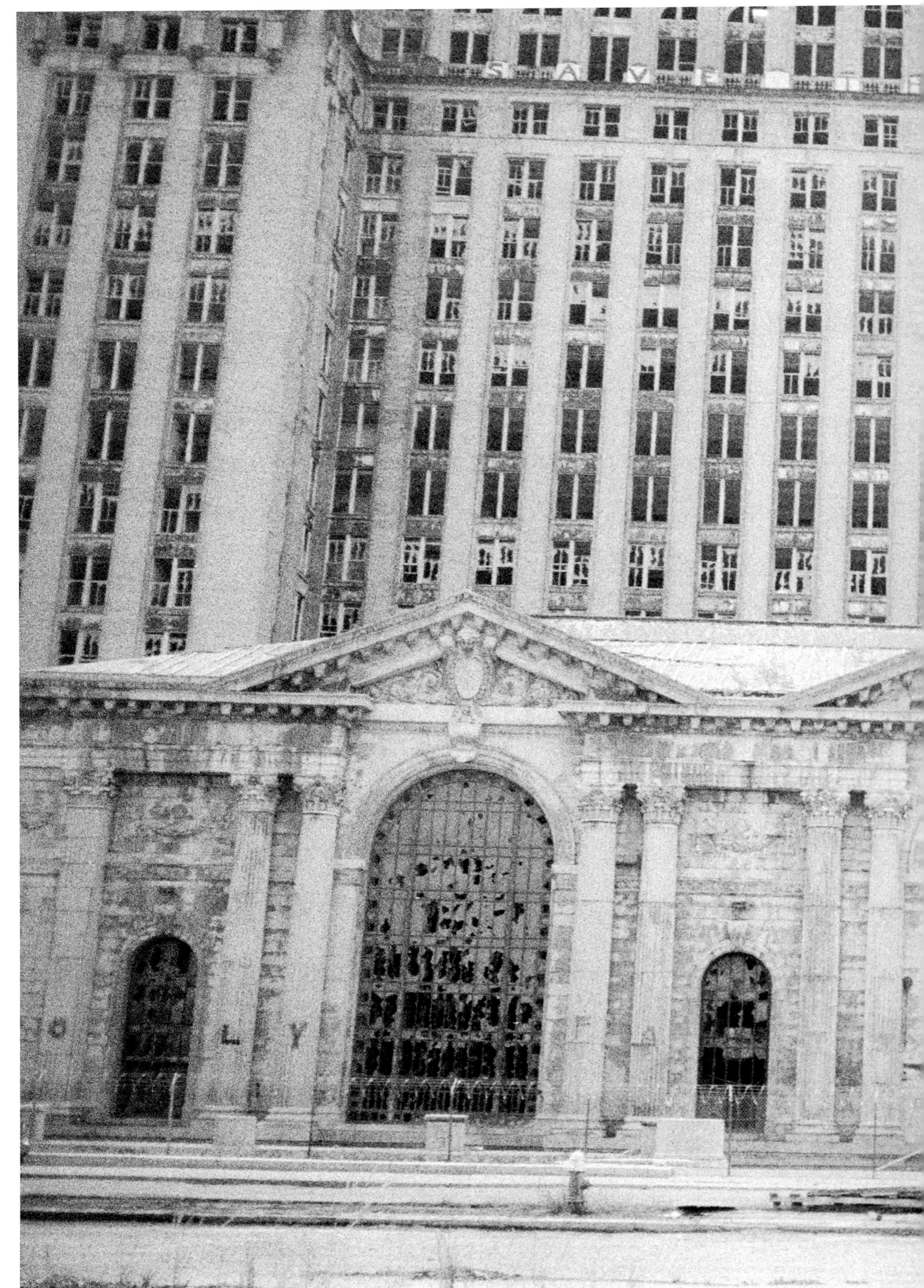

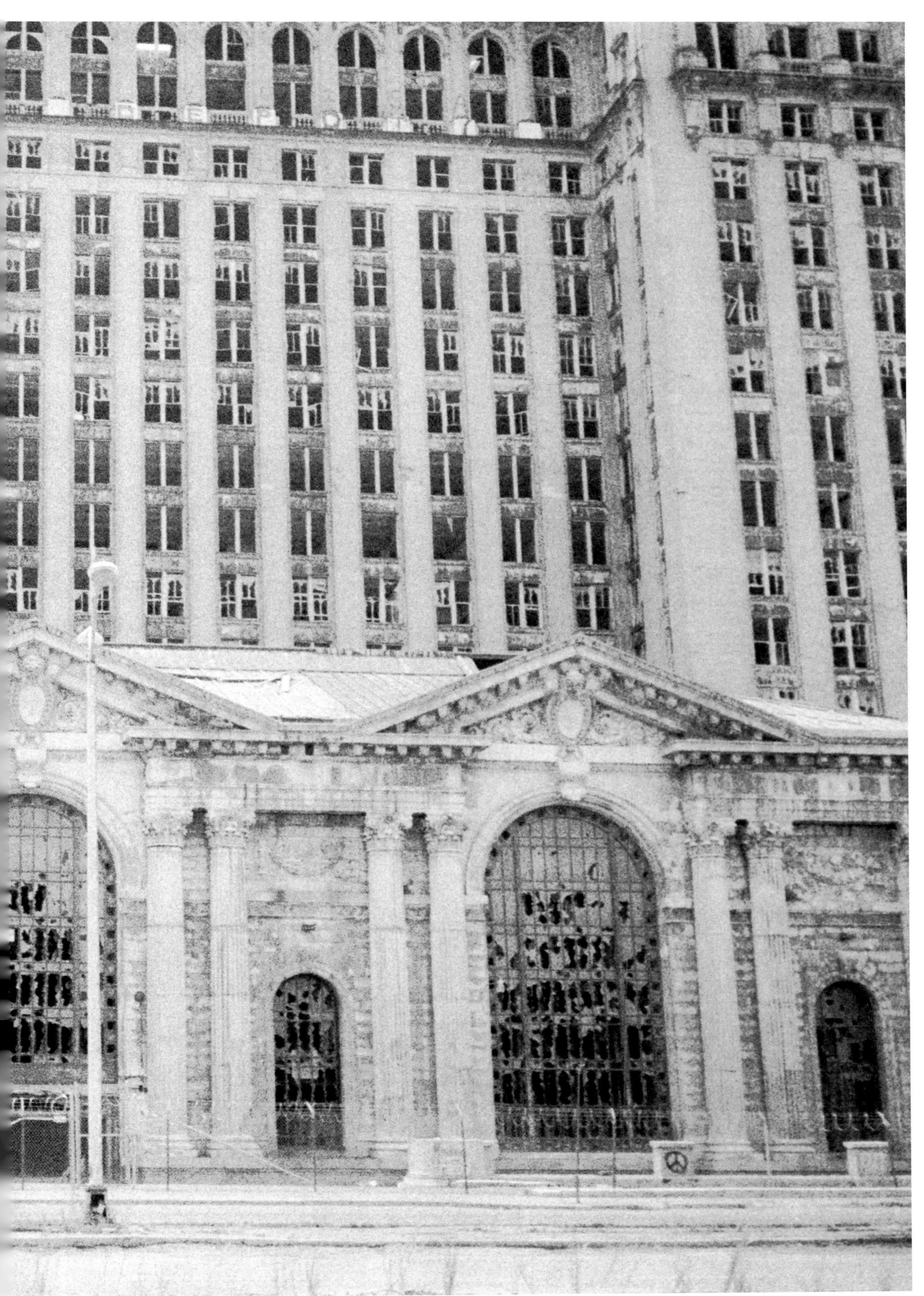

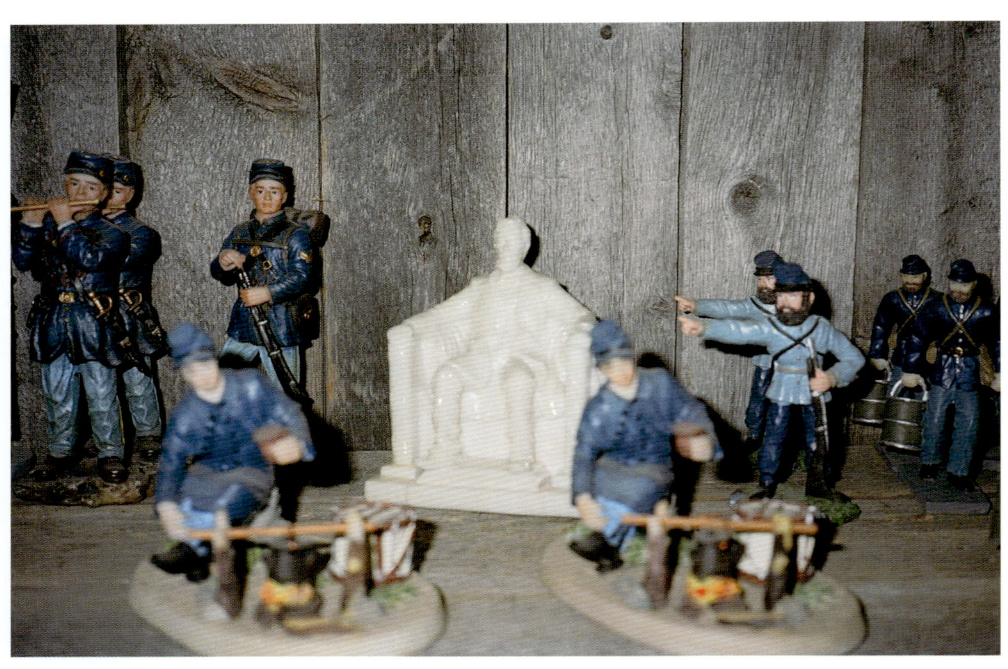

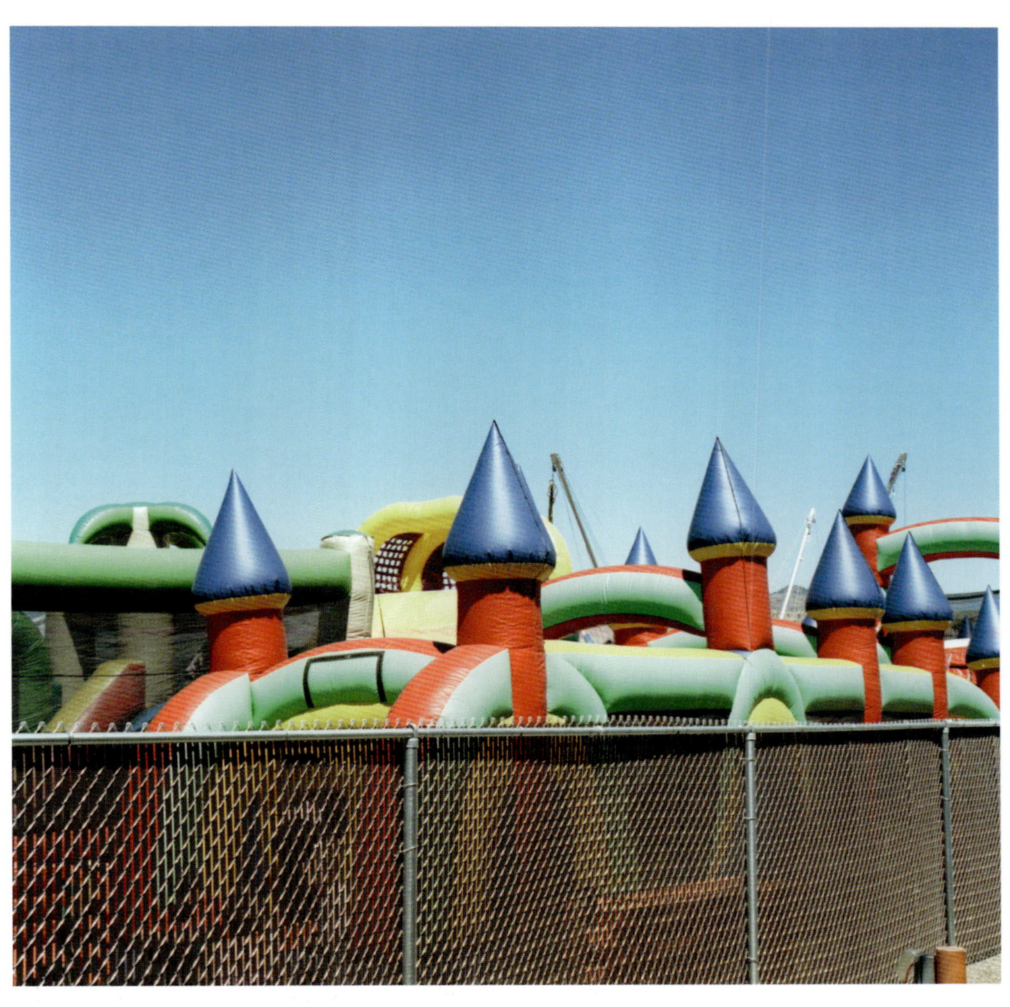

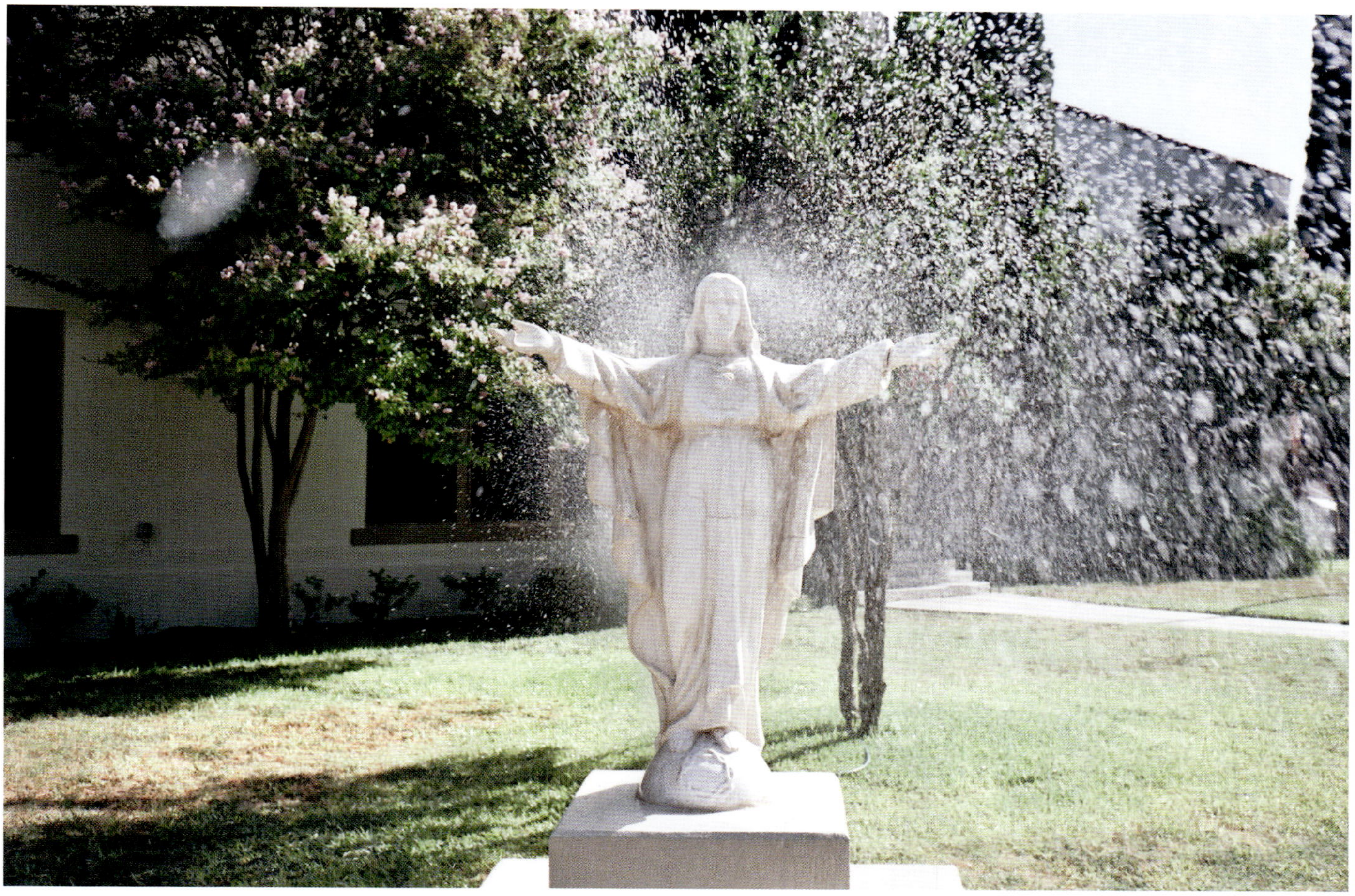

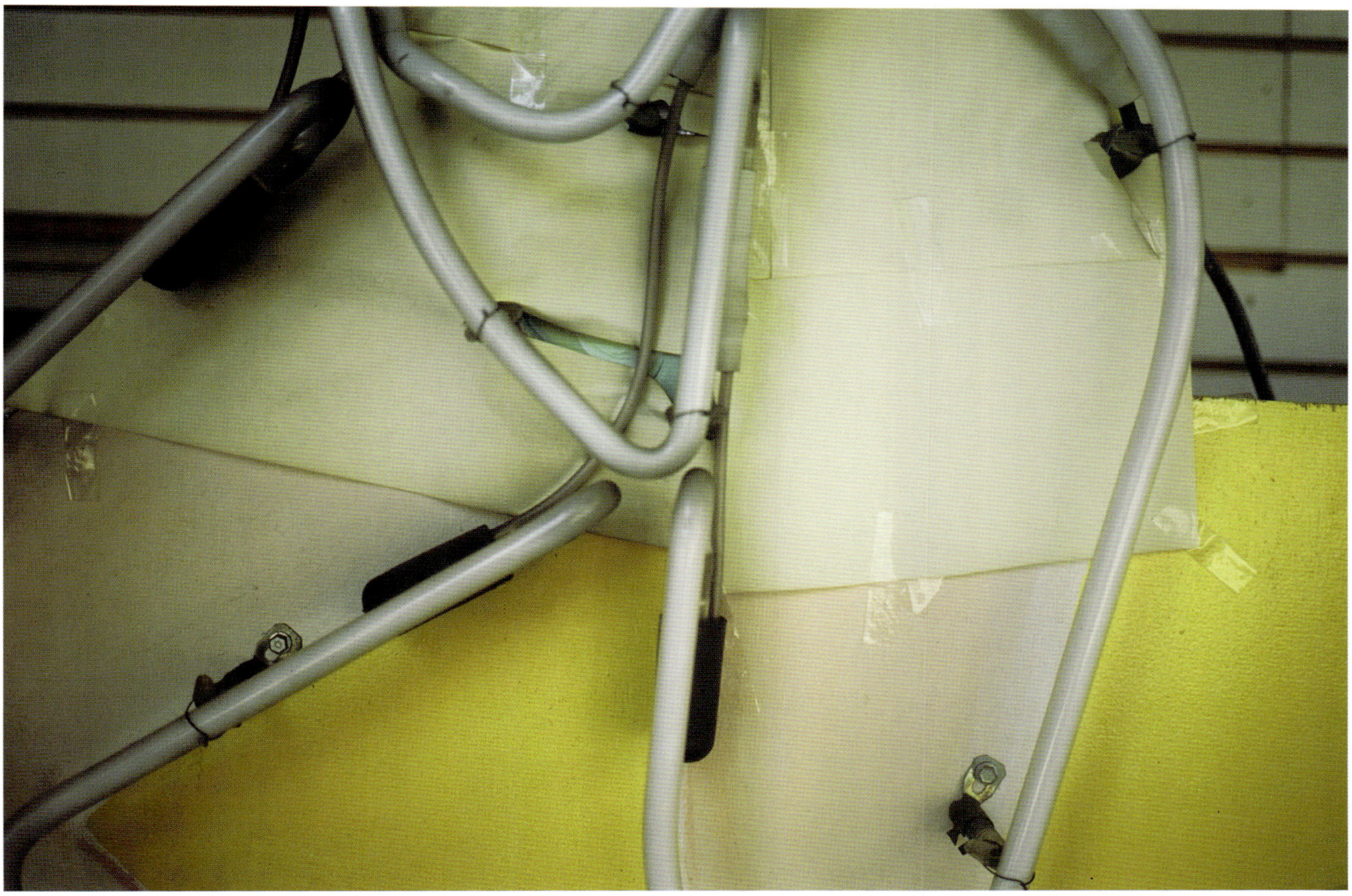

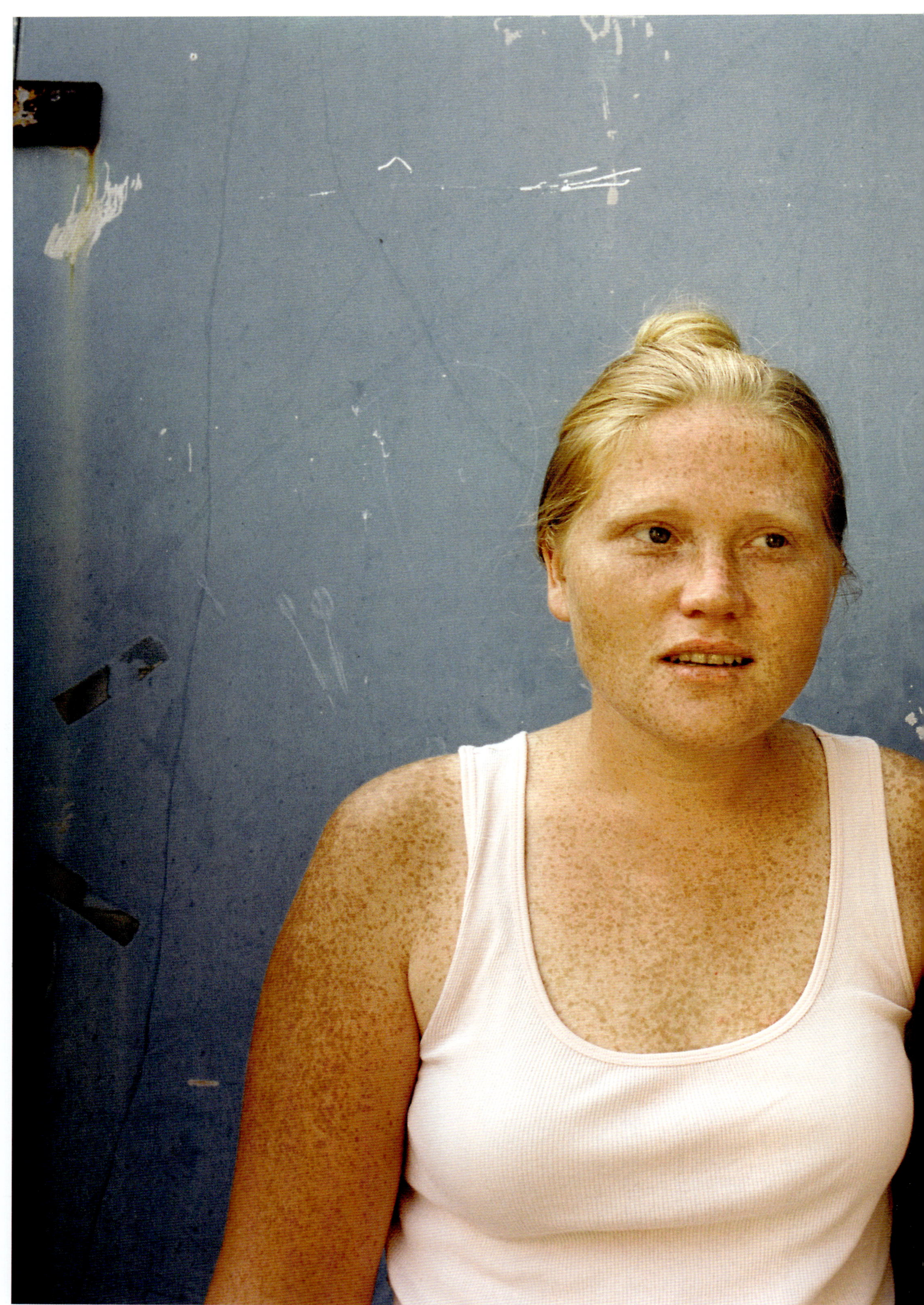

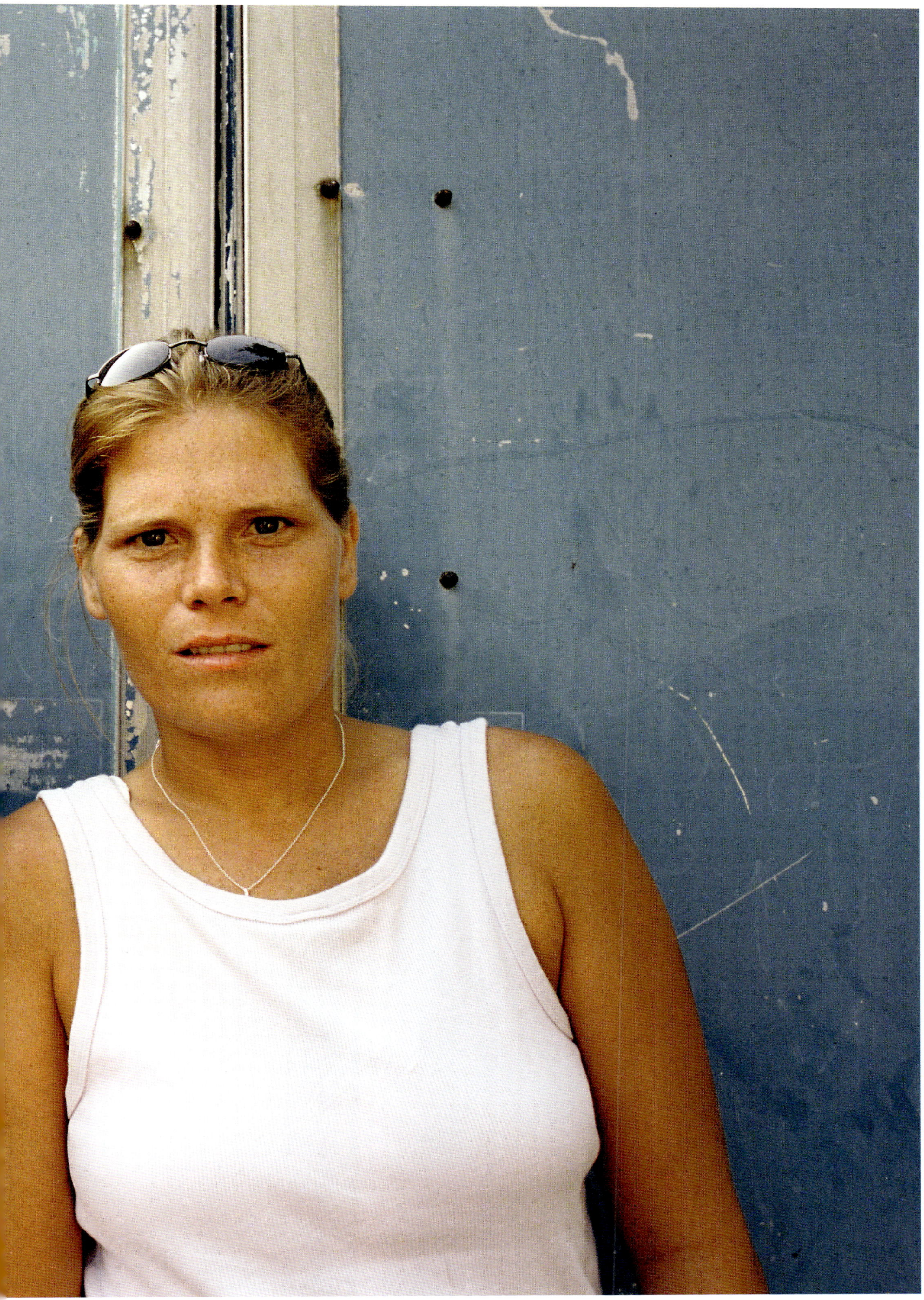

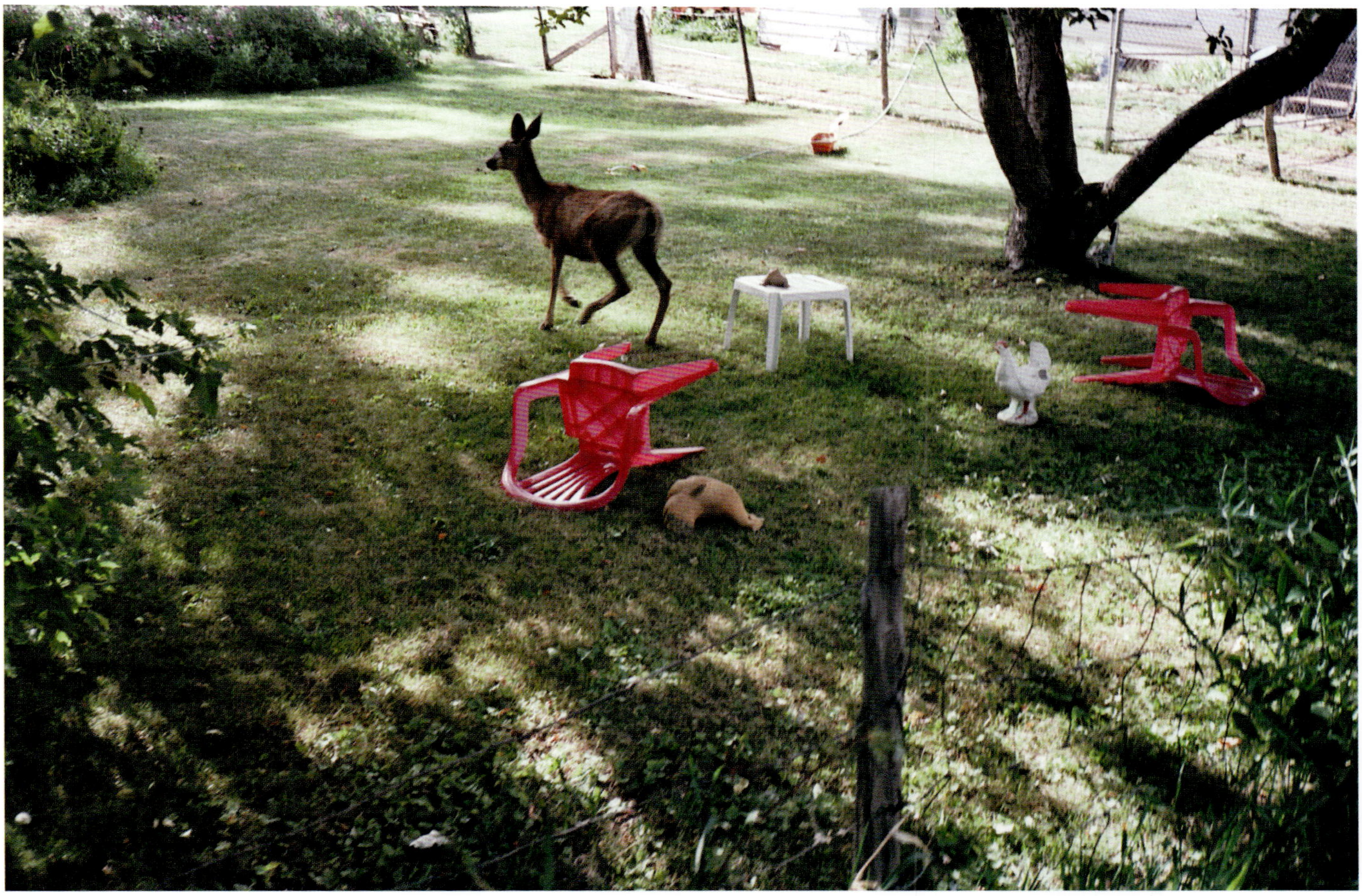

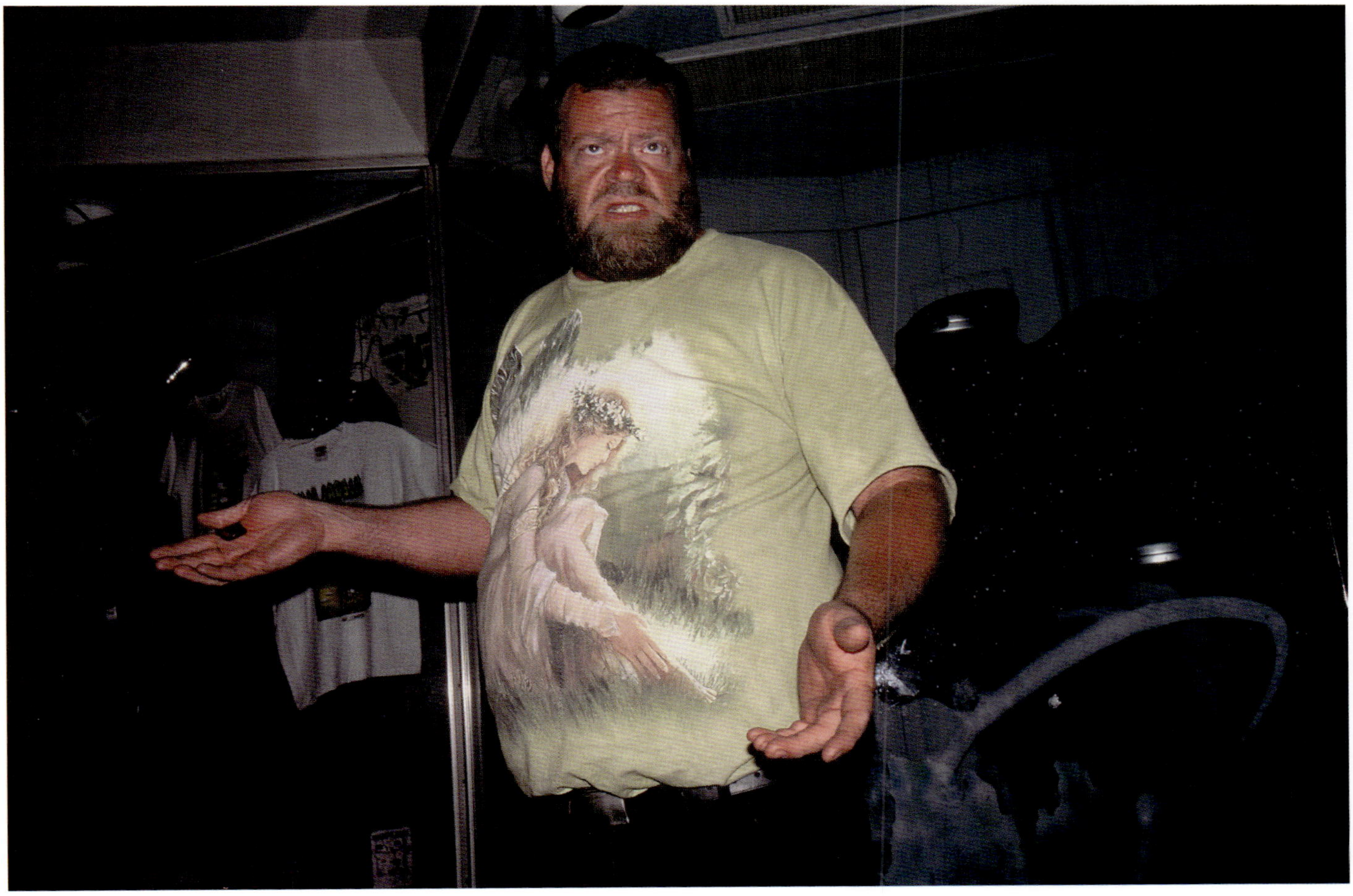

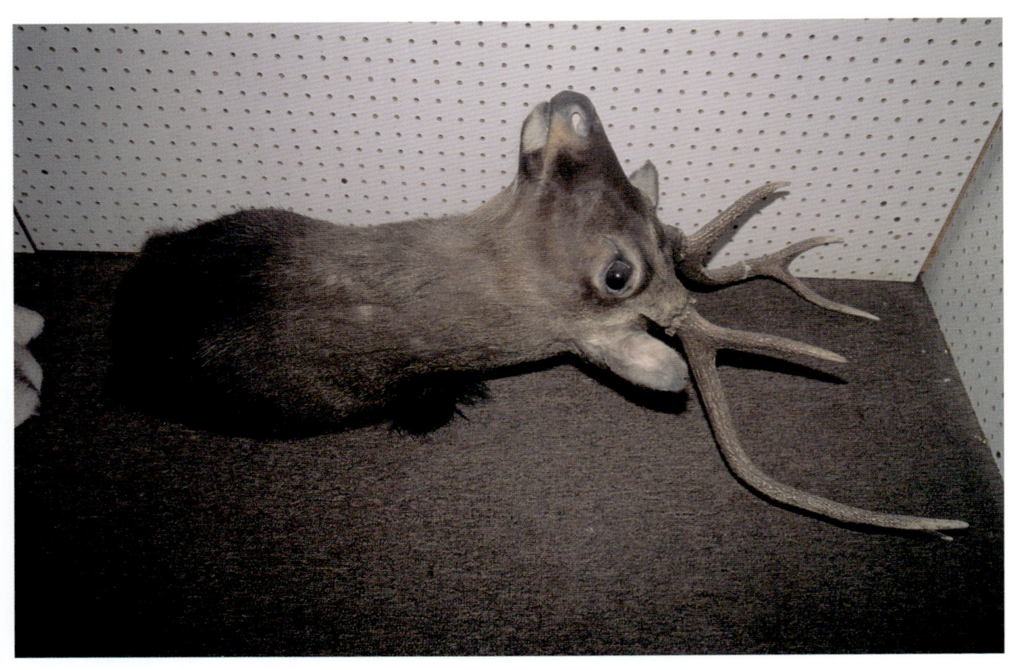

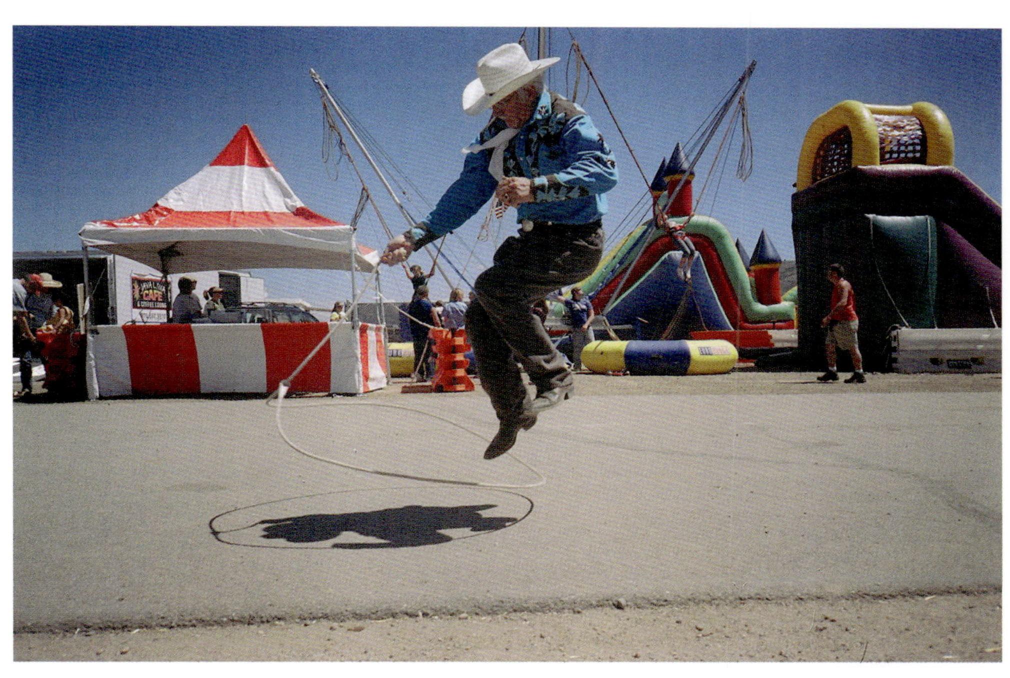

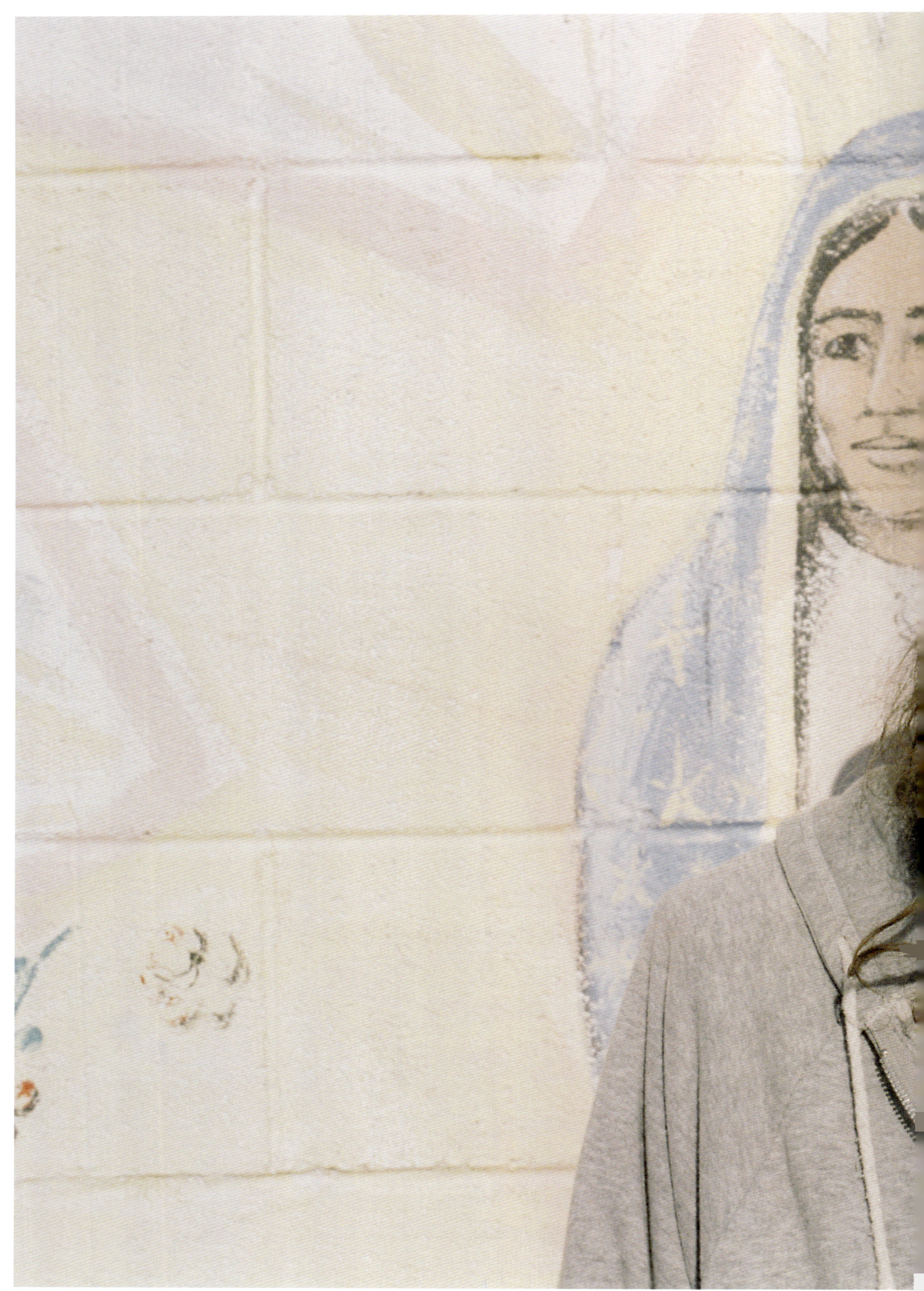

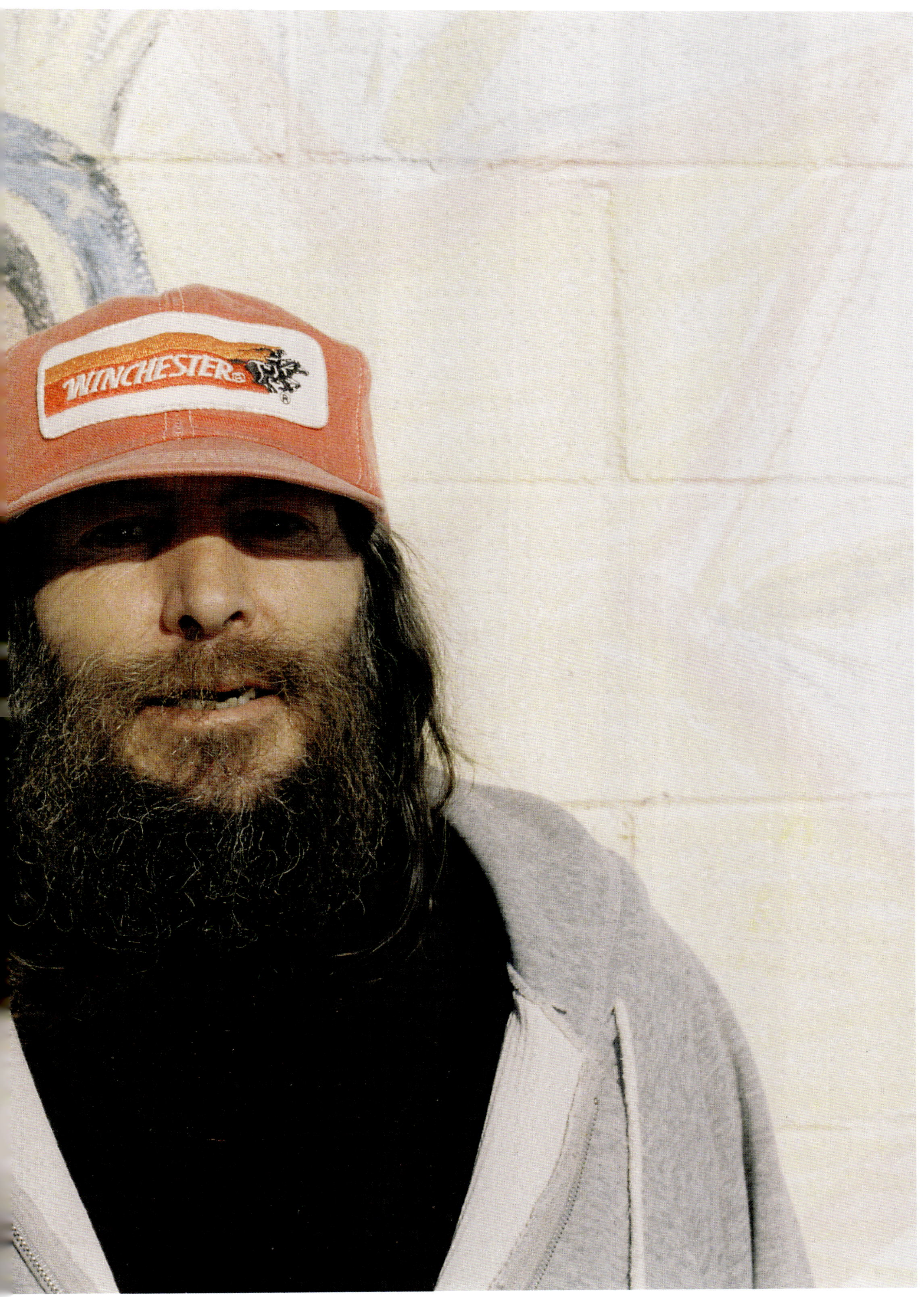
WINCHESTER

Attendant Figures:
An Introduction to the work of Acree, Eaton and Johnson.
By Matthew Hall.

In opening a discourse of the image, its constellation, and its apprehension, reproduction and application, such as we have in the book, *Coney Island Malibu Beach*, it will serve well to express a prefatory statement regarding the collation and composition of images.

This book gathers together a series of photographs taken by Benjamin Acree, Jackson Eaton and Robert S. Johnson, as they collectively passed through the United States in 2009. What is striking in these images is the very absence of the cultivated, dominant images, we all, as everyday consumers of imagery and photography, have as archetypes of Malibu Beach: there are no glimmering building facades, no sun-baked, oil-glistening skin, no lines of palm trees in crepuscular light. It is this absence that defines the collection; an absence which does not attempt to signify the sanctity of the condition, but provides, determinedly, its own portrait of the Real. What is significant in the collection is the ability of the group to capture and represent motion. Knowing of the road trip that gave life to these images before having seen the images themselves, lent to my own reading a portion of that collective, shared experience of travel and an incentive to read the works in a combinatorial, evolving, revelational pattern. This is a landscape that I also have travelled, quite independent of the photographers, and at a much earlier age, so I too came into my experience of the book with my own pattern of images, memories, and thoughts from which to read them, my own distant histories.

The patterning of images which constellate the book is experienced through the manner in which each photographer has added something concordant, something intrepid, of his own experience to the collection. There is an aesthetic contiguity which unites these images and representations of the world, yet also something decidedly gravid and expressive of an individual posessivity in each photograph. There is a collective, shared and assumed risk which resonates through the collation of the photographs by Eaton, Acree and Johnson. The book possesses what the German philosopher Theodor Adorno called a Verständigung, a mutual understanding; the collaboration between photographers and this symbiotic relationship heightens the reader's apprehension of the images; it is a shared and collective journey where each participant is invited to partake in the resonances of the experience.[1] The book speaks of and to the possibilities of a shared experience; it constellates the images of shared apprehension, a shared understanding and asks the viewer to engage with the tactile and virile surfaces encountered in a trip across the United States.

What is particularly resonant within this collection is the idea of representing motion, of the energy and the possibilities of representing momentum and movement in a single image and in a series of images. In Gilles Deleuze's book, *Francis Bacon: The Logic of Sensation*, Deleuze articulates a theory for reading the images of the painter in a manner in which the inherent properties of motion are detailed in the relationship between images. For Deleuze, it was the "forced movement" or "rhythms" which constituted the dialectic possibilities

---

1 Adorno, T. W., with Max Horkheimer. *Dialectic of Enlightenment*. Trans. Edmund Jephcott. Stanford: Stanford UP, 2002. 242.

of apprehending the true Figure, or true experience of the triptychs of Bacon.[2] This theory has application in a reading of Acree, Johnson and Eaton's collated works as well. In reading the series of images, their combinatorial values and meanings change in much the manner that Deleuze described: they set on with steady or 'attendant' rhythms; an active rising, or diastolic rhythm; and a passive, descending or systolic rhythm.[3] It is the complex formed through the layering of the photographs' values and meanings that provide the true means of assessment, a true method by which to read the text subsumed behind the images. This collection of photographs articulates the possibility of narrative and experience through the rhythm of its disclosures. The multiplicity of meanings encourages an engagement which is equally intimate, inviting and disturbing.

In *Coney Island Malibu Beach*, the collection remains highly cognisant of this attendant rhythm, while subverting expectations of the popularised image of America. Indeed it is the very disconsolate and discordant imagery which suggests the collection's radical alterity, its attendance and absorption of the imperfect, the unfamiliar, the worn, and the uncanny in the everyday, which makes this collection remarkable. Following on from the photographers' lead of using a quotation from Susan Sontag as an epigraph, I would suggest that this book represents a registering, a mapping, it represents coming to an understanding of the discordant in the everyday through the use of photography. Sontag wrote that "photographs... help people to take possession of space in which they are insecure." [4] The logical extension of this insecurity, this uncertainty, marginalisation, or alienation, can be found in the collection *Coney Island Malibu Beach*, which juxtaposes images of the discord and surrealistic exposition of everyday American life. Forgone are the skyscrapers and palm trees, the glittering cars and highly attenuated image-reflecting windows of shop fronts and what confronts the viewer is a scarred, tattooed back; lonely vacant looks; the remnants of a religious fervour. What one confronts in these images is a glimpse of the Real. Further on in Sontag's book, *On Photography*, is a quotation which is quite stunningly appropriate in a book which represents passing through the demesne of the iconographic image, "Insofar as photography does peel away the dry wrappers of habitual seeing, it creates another habit of seeing, both intense and cool, solicitous and detached; charmed by the insignificant detail; addicted to incongruity."[5] This quotation defines much of what can be found in the book, its cultivation and production of images; the book speaks to the conditions of the Real, it speaks to the discord of everyday life.

Carrying our cognitive thread forward from Deleuze, let us consider these images and their collective production as a movement from "the synthesis of perception (apprehension, reproduction, recognition) to aesthetic comprehension (rhythm) to the catastrophe (chaos) and back again: the painter passes through a catastrophe (the diagram) and in the process produces a form of a completely different nature (the Figure)."[6] The vectors of motion which define speed and momentum, eastward or westward, across the vast fields of the United States entail and are defined by a fundamental violence. Just as the painter starts with a diagram, the photographers started with a map, pencil marks showing directions, a legend scrawled over a tangle of overpasses and sidetracks, straight into the heart of the country. The photographers in this case never presume the unfamiliar, they reveal it, they have passed through the catastrophe, they have borne witness to violence of everyday life and have amassed it before us. They have given this to us, through their experiences, through their own habits of seeing. They have experienced it and have laid out their attendant Figures in this book. As befitting the photographs, Sontag provides what is ultimately a fulsome description of the art of image-making: "Photography is an elegiac art, a twilight art. Most subjects photographed are, just by virtue of being photographed, touched with pathos."[7] This book, for me, entails a summation of that vision; it is a vision of the pathos of America, an attendant vision of art.

---

2 Deleuze, Gilles. Francis Bacon: *The Logic of Sensation. Trans.* Daniel W. Smith. Minneapolis University of Minnesota Press, 2002. 51.

3 Ibid. 55, and adapted from Smith's introduction xv.

4 Sontag, Susan. On Photography. New York: Farrar, Straus and Giroux, 1977. 9.

5 Ibid. 100.

6 Deleuze, Gilles. *Francis Bacon: The Logic of Sensation.* From Smith's introduction 'Deleuze on Bacon: Three Conceptual Trajectories in The Logic of Sensation'. xx.

7 Sontag, Susan. On Photography. 15

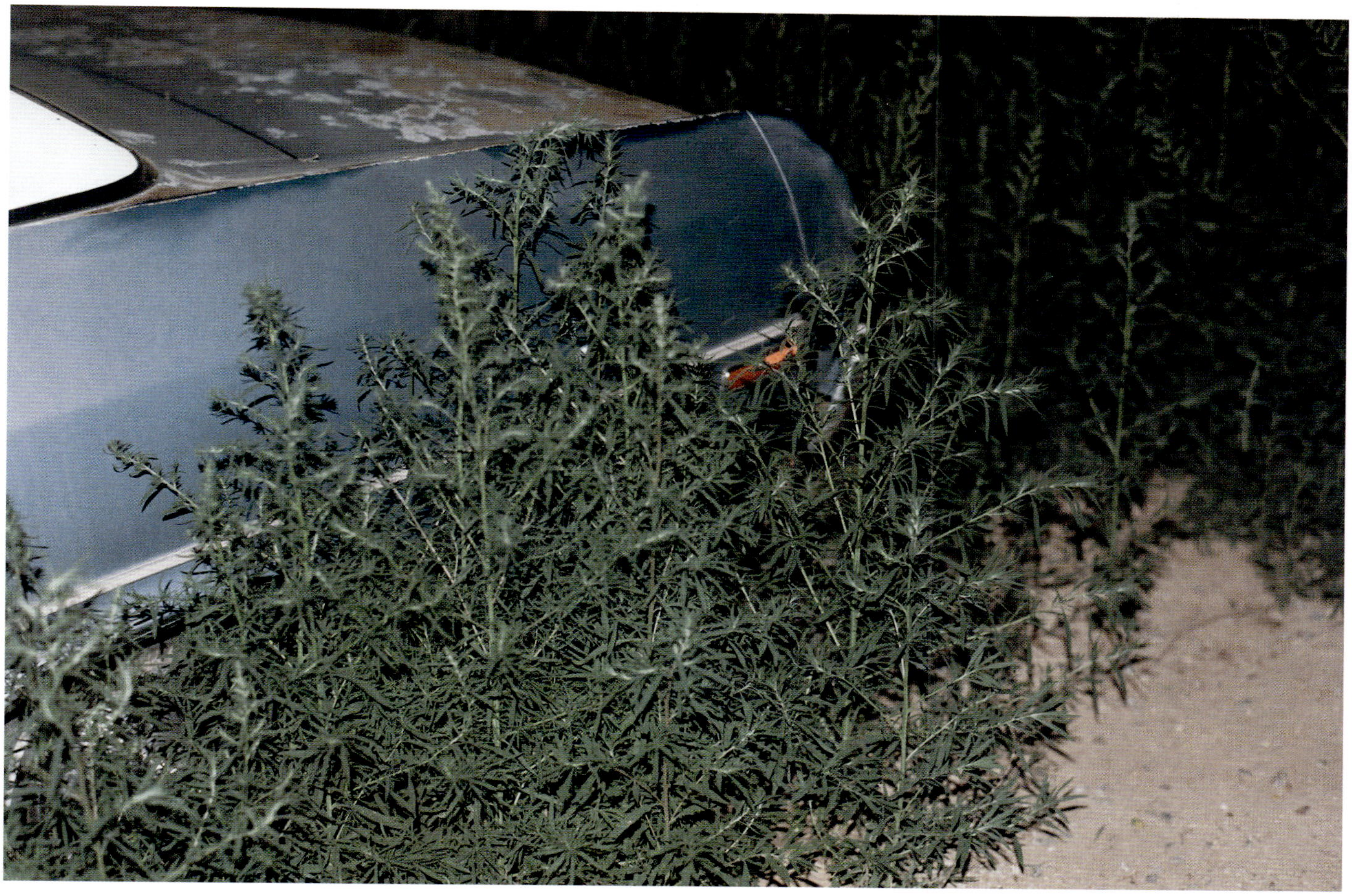

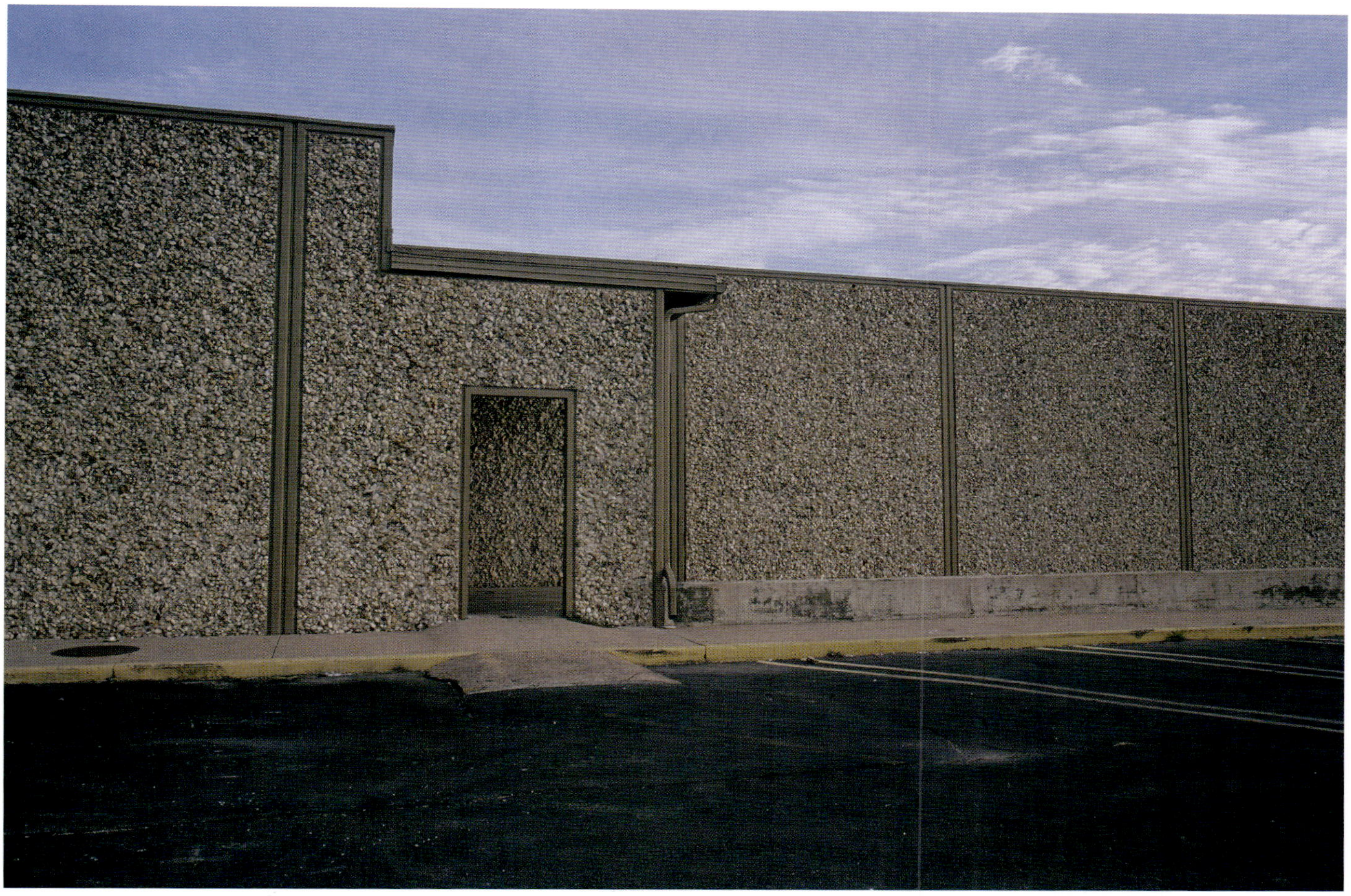

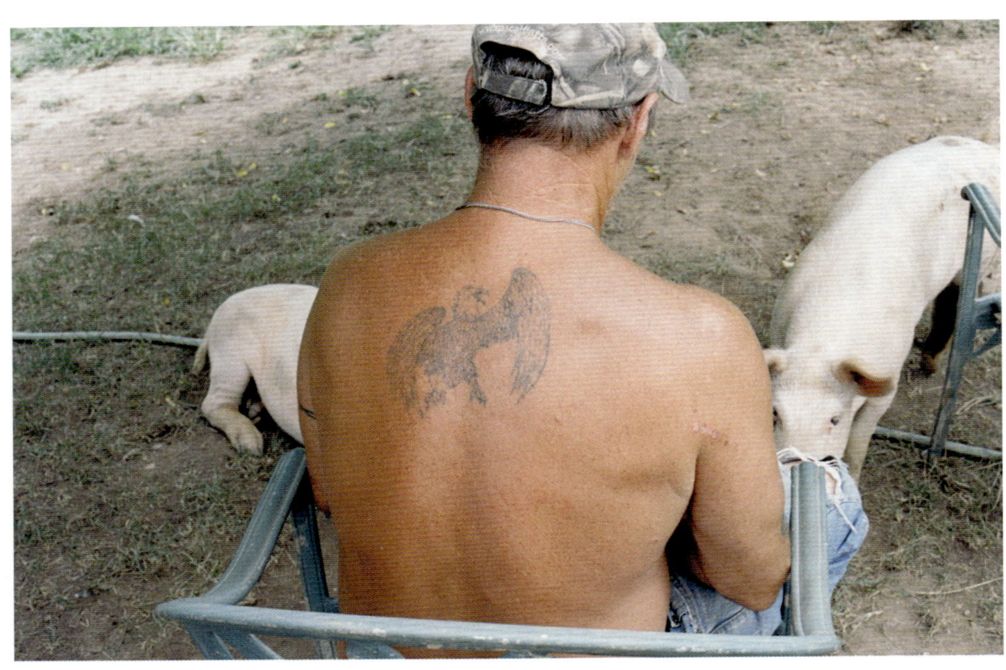

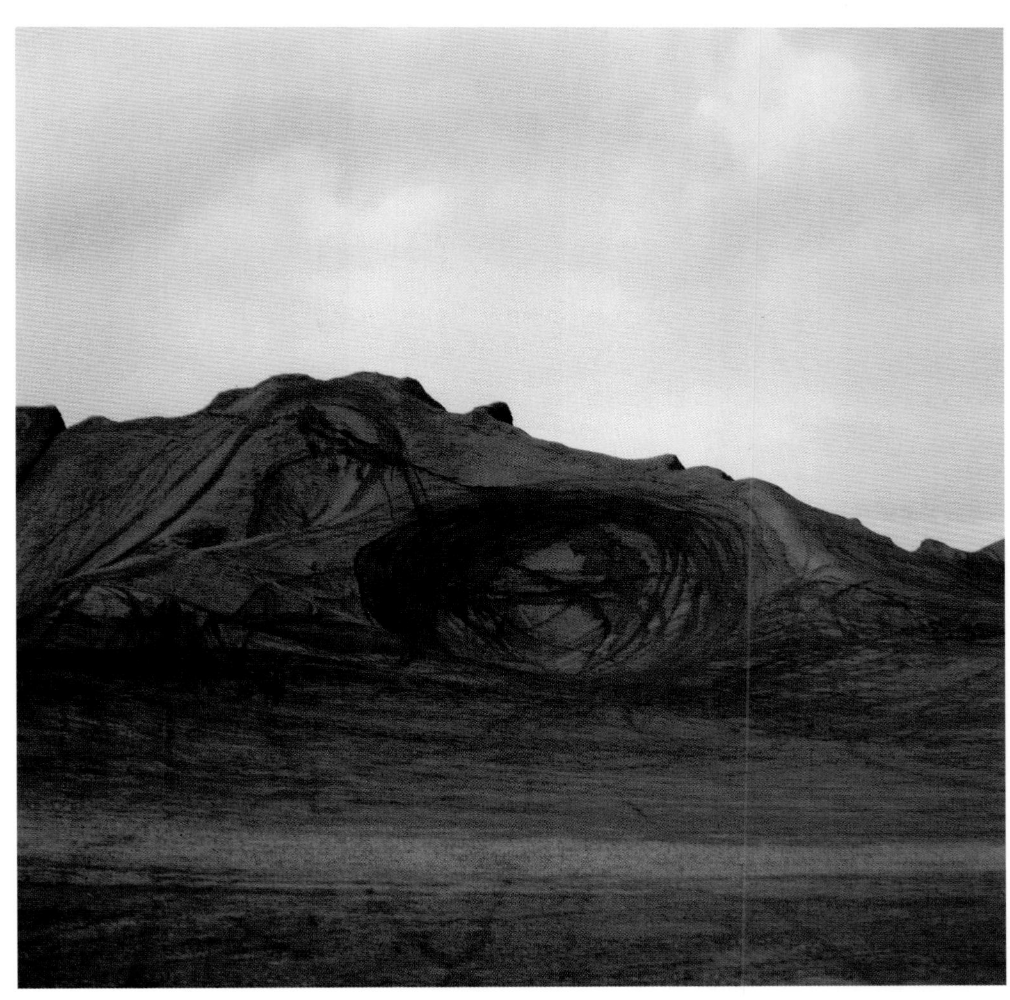

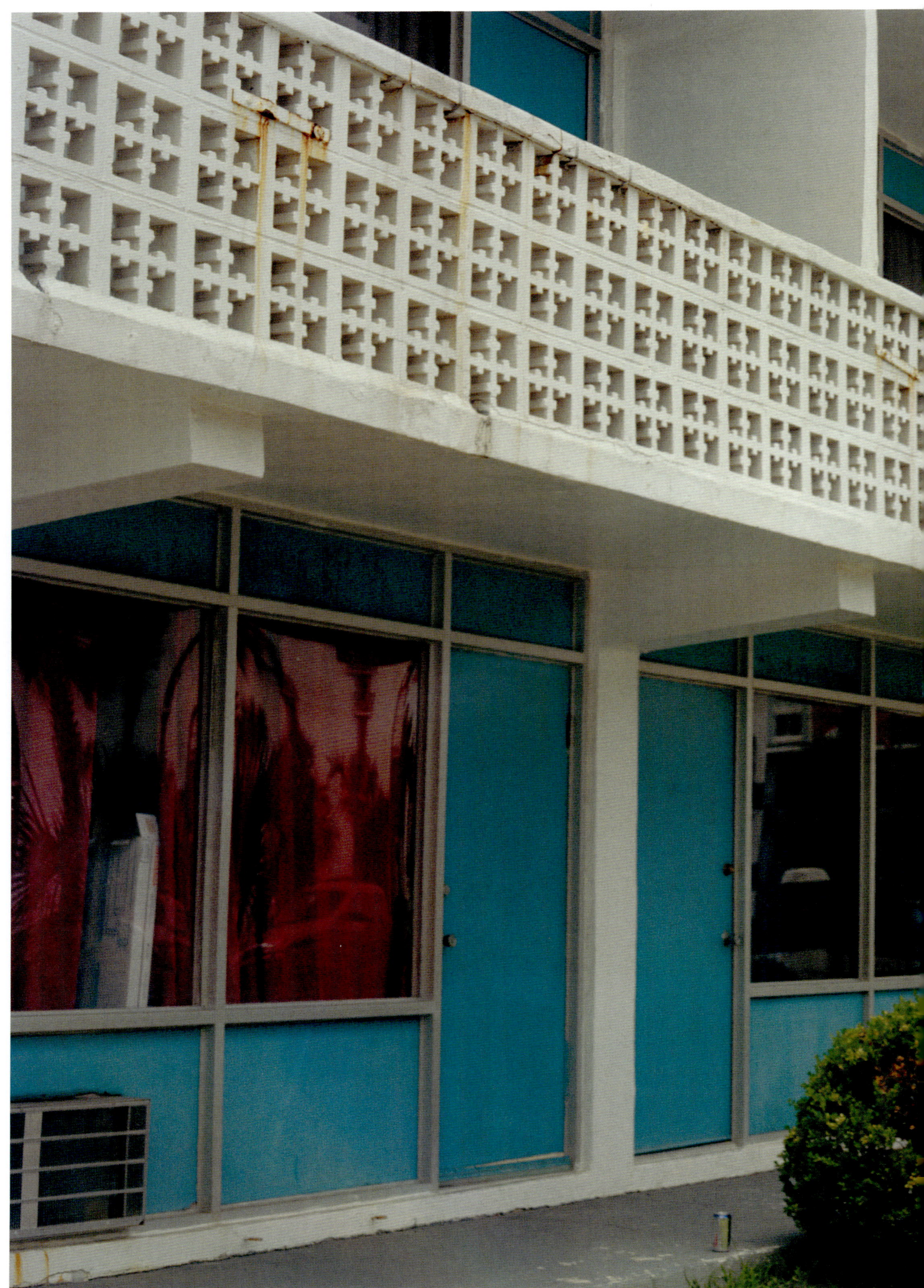

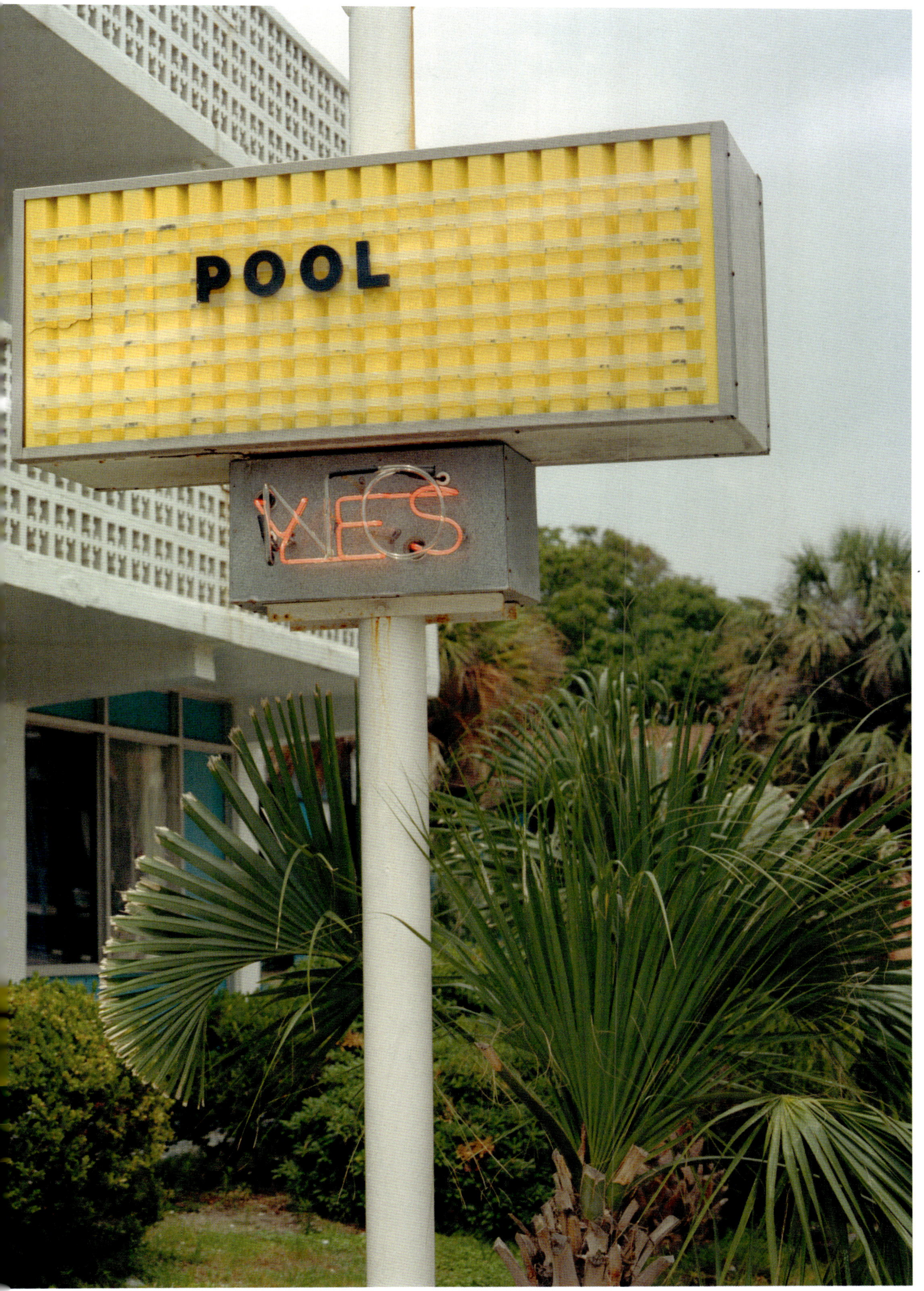
POOL
YES

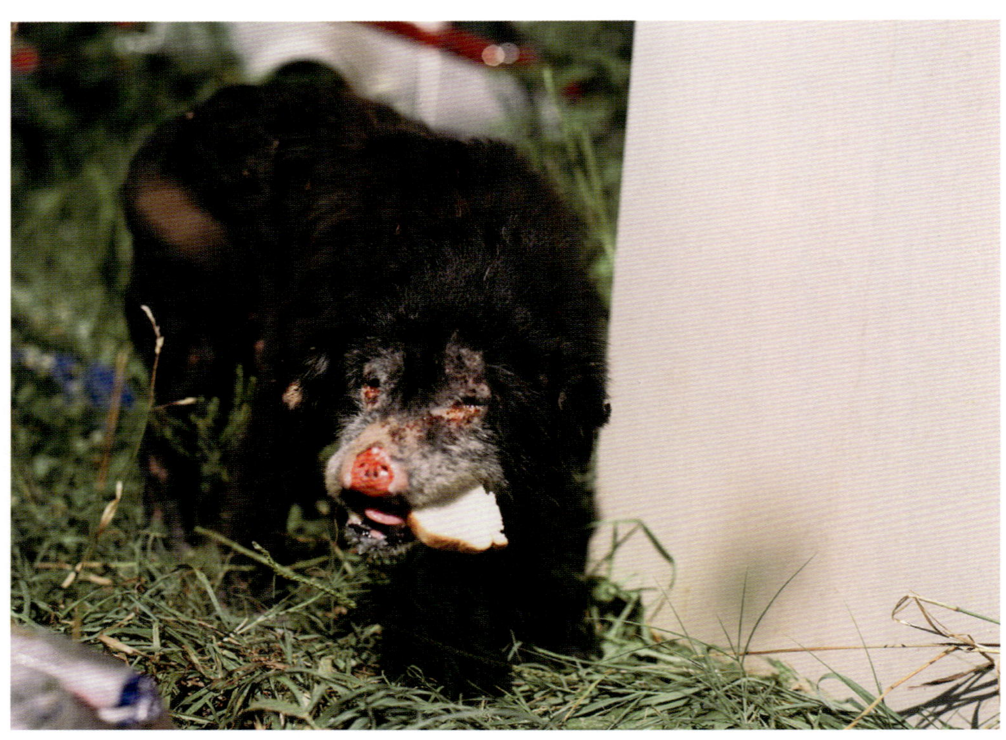

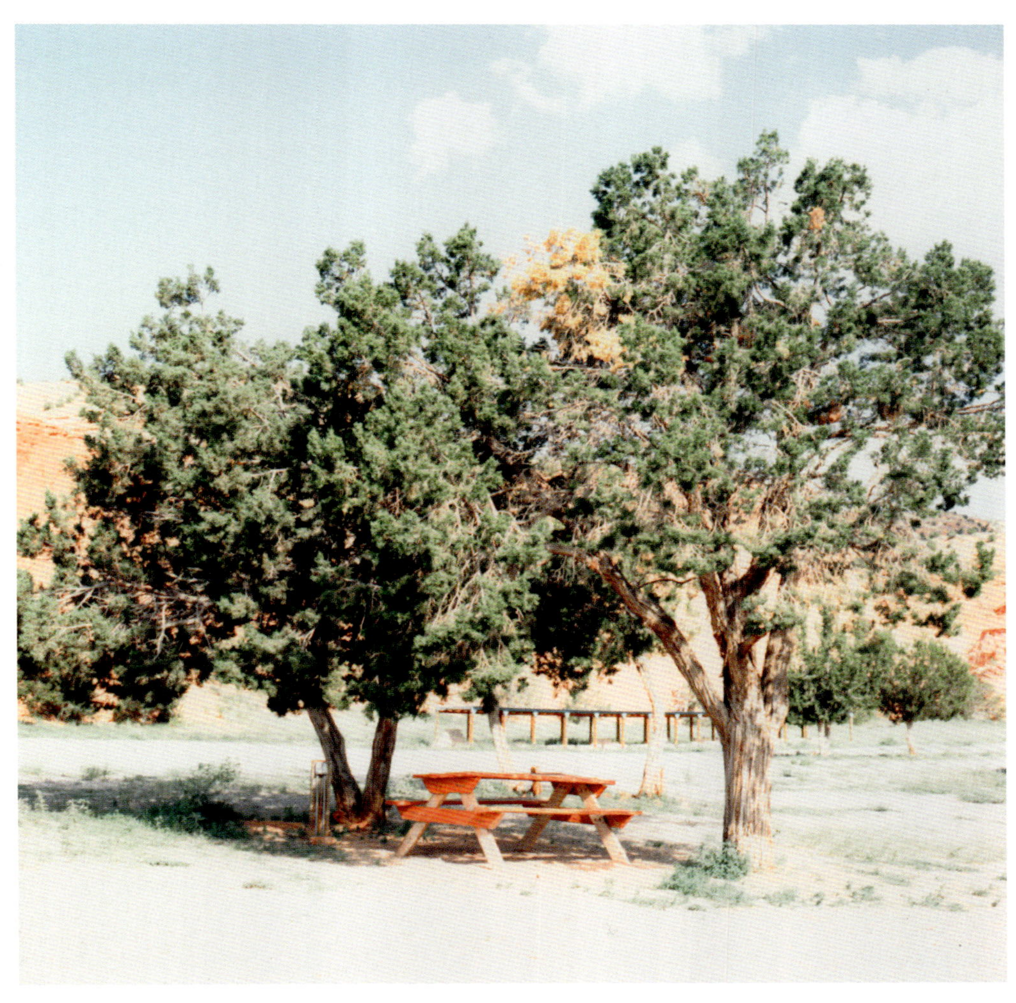

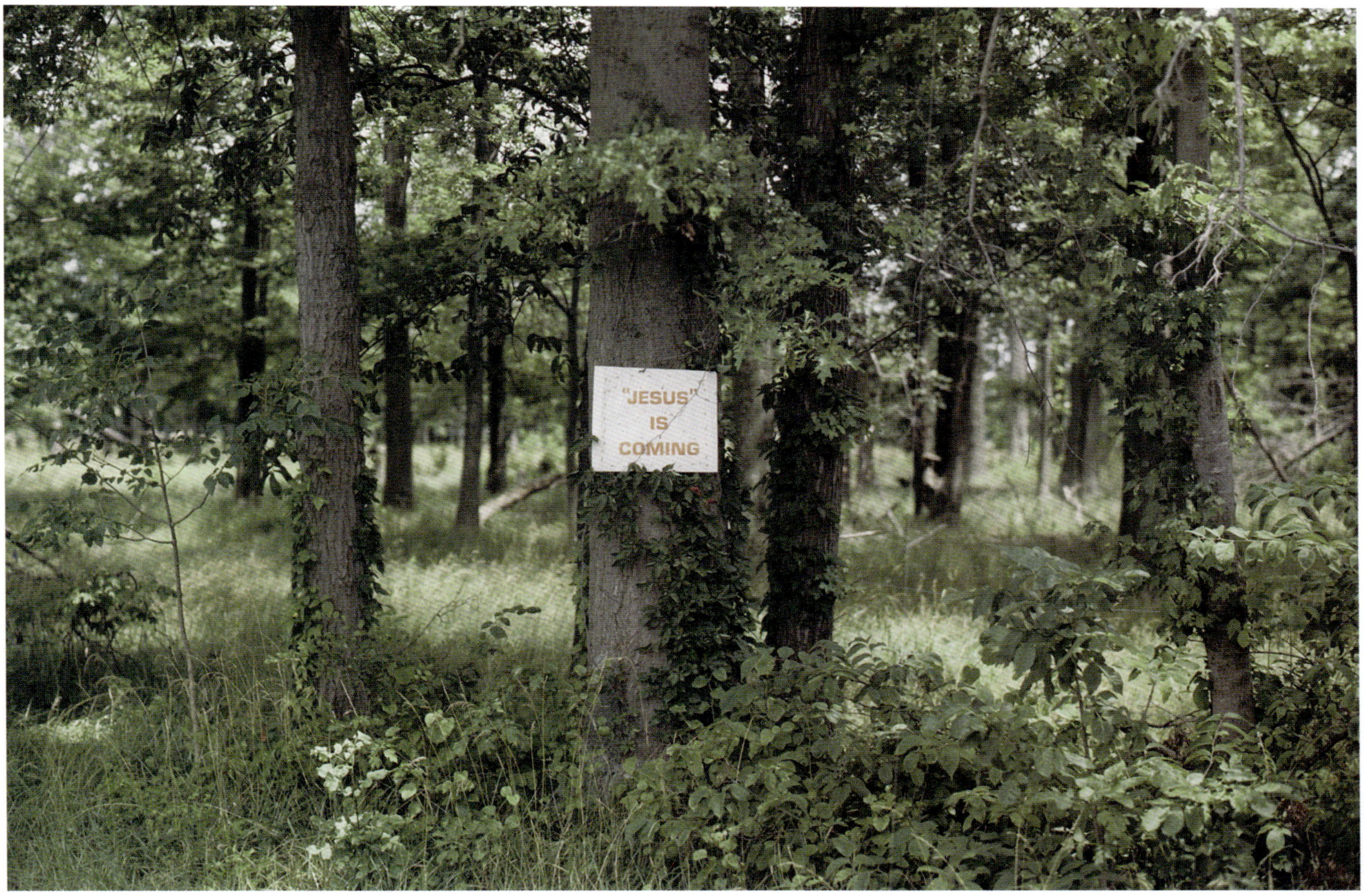

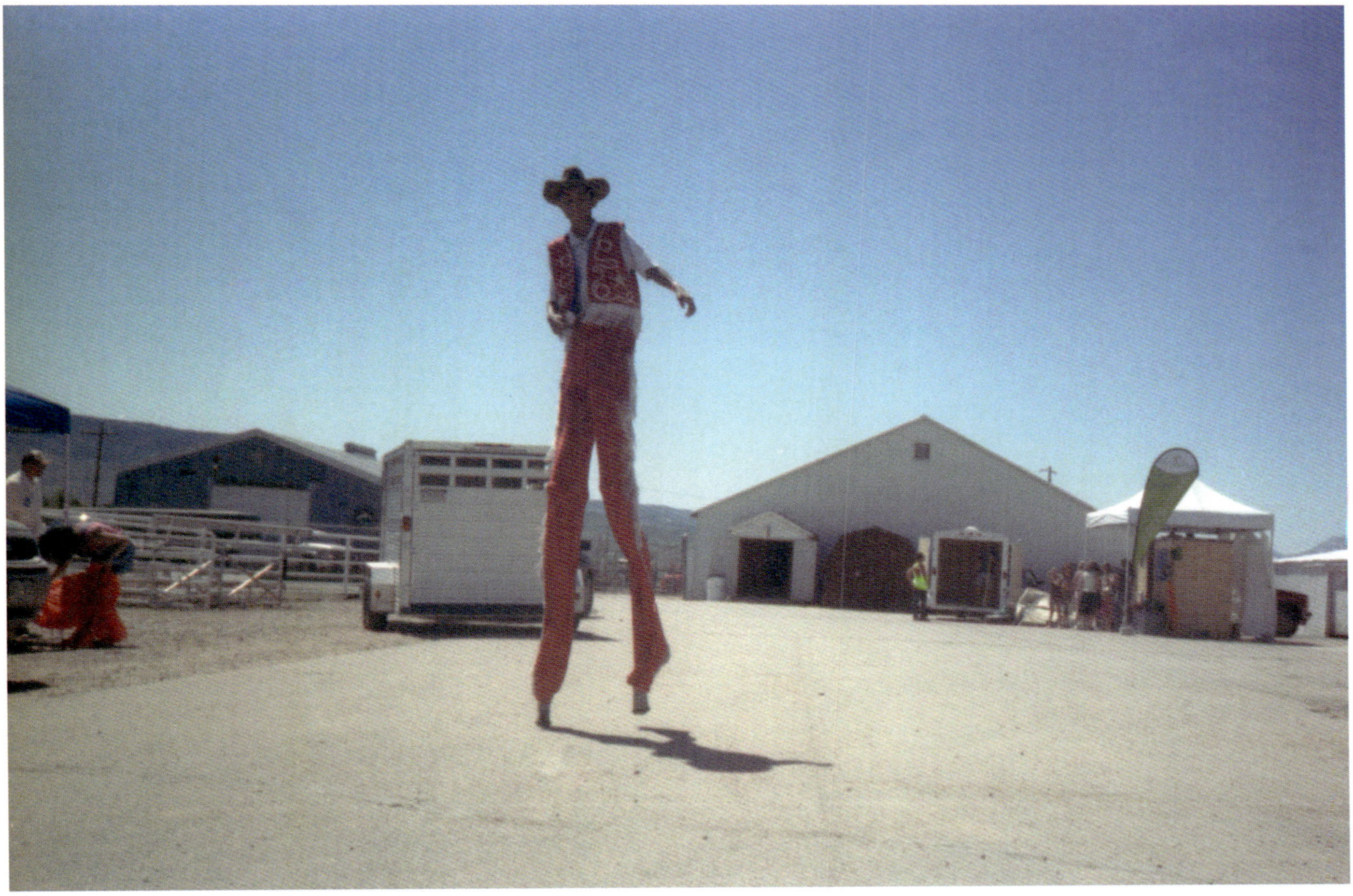

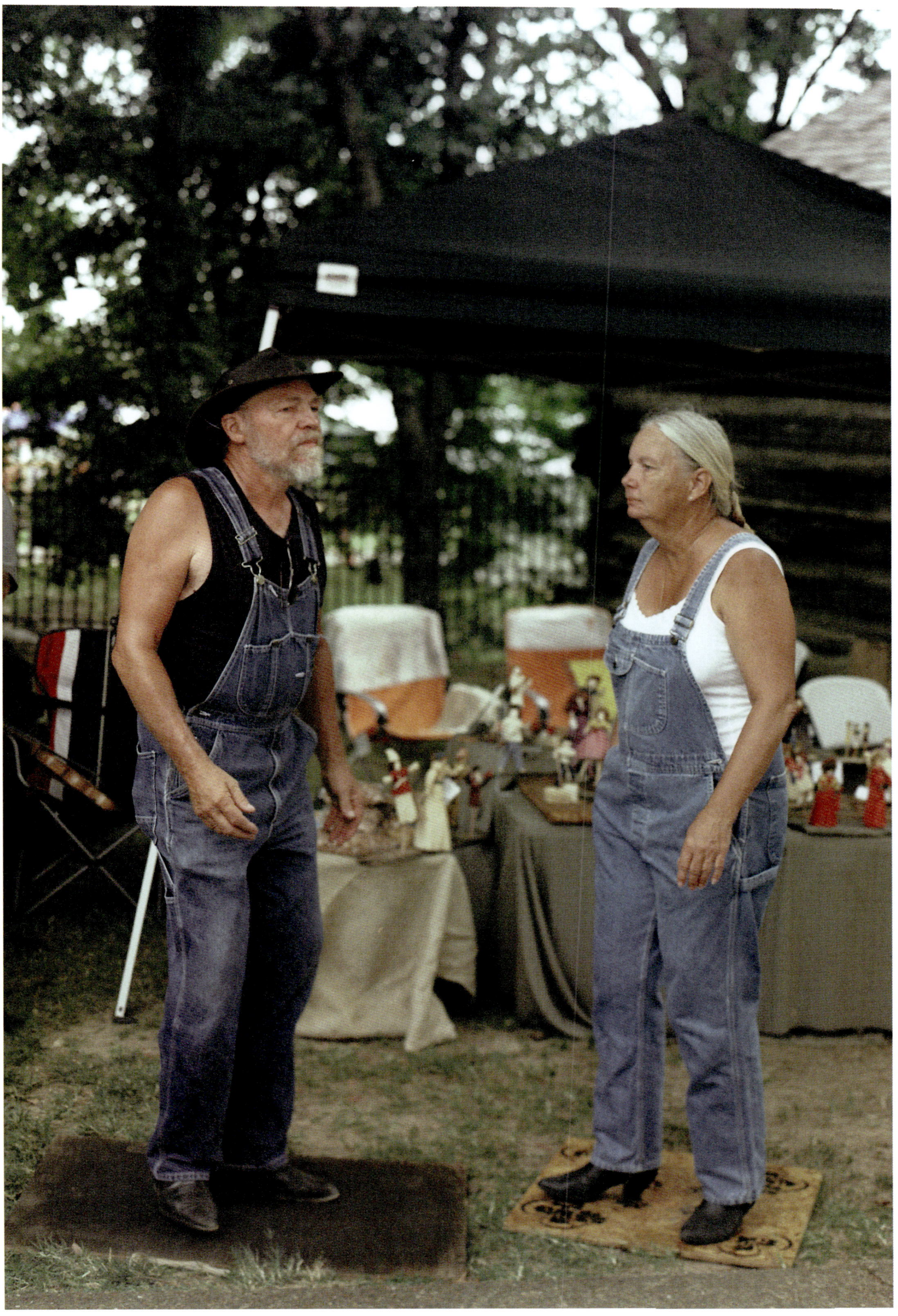

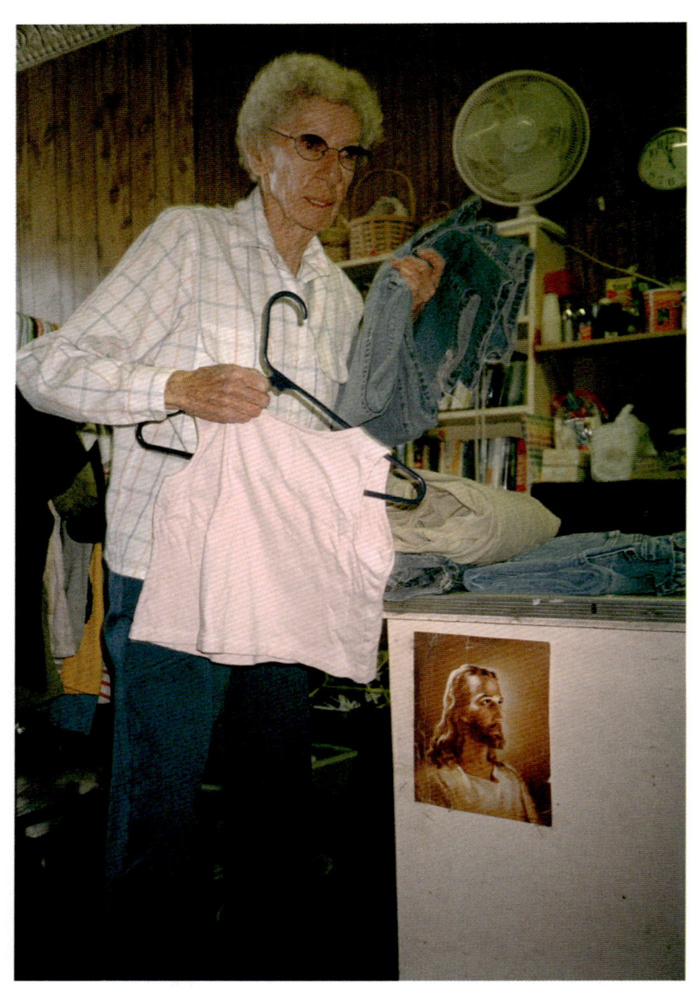

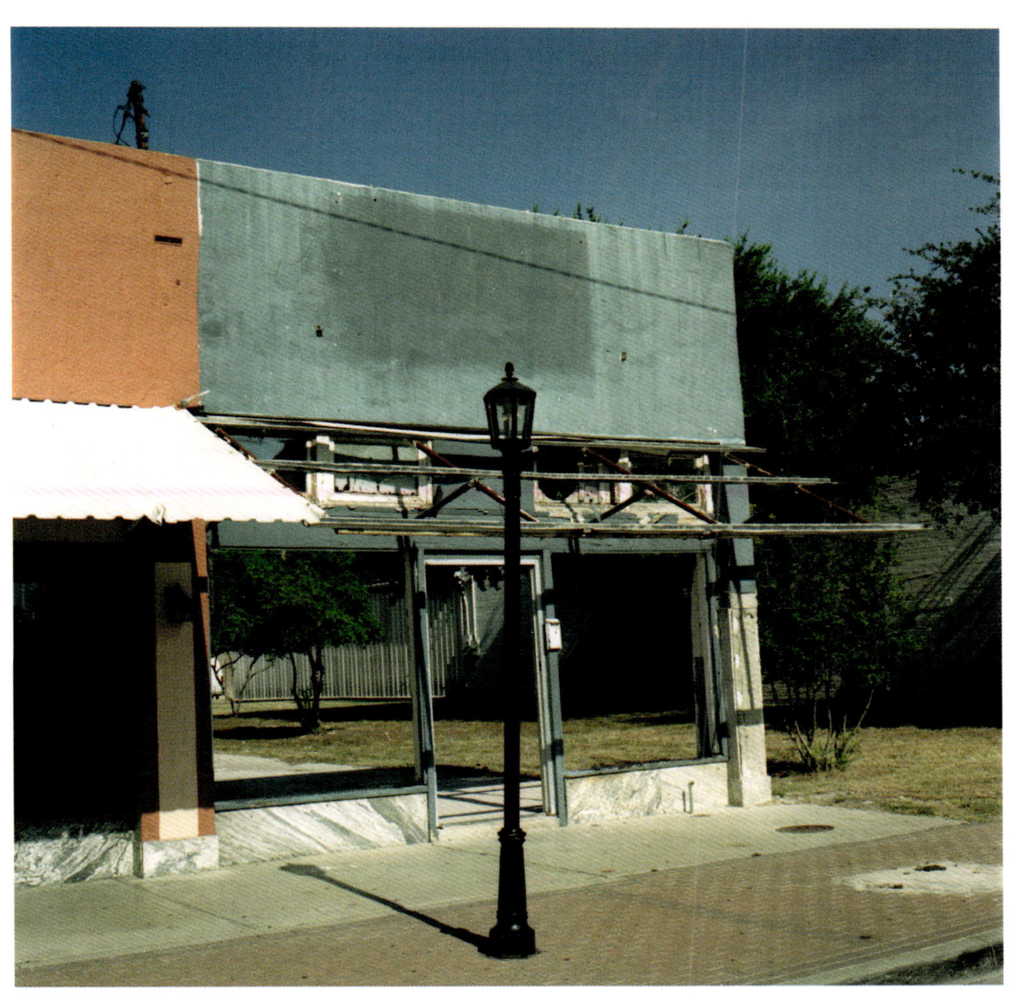

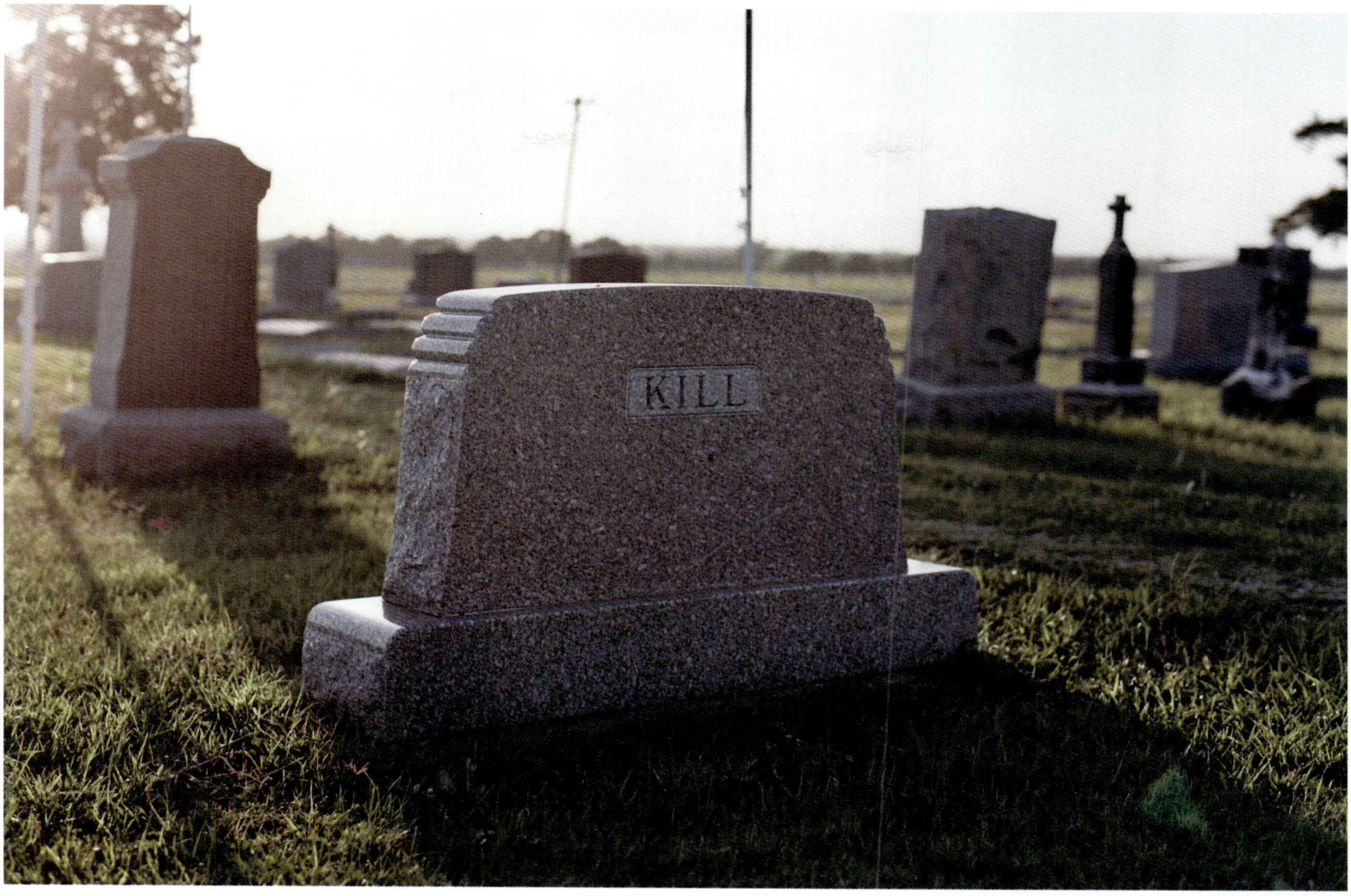

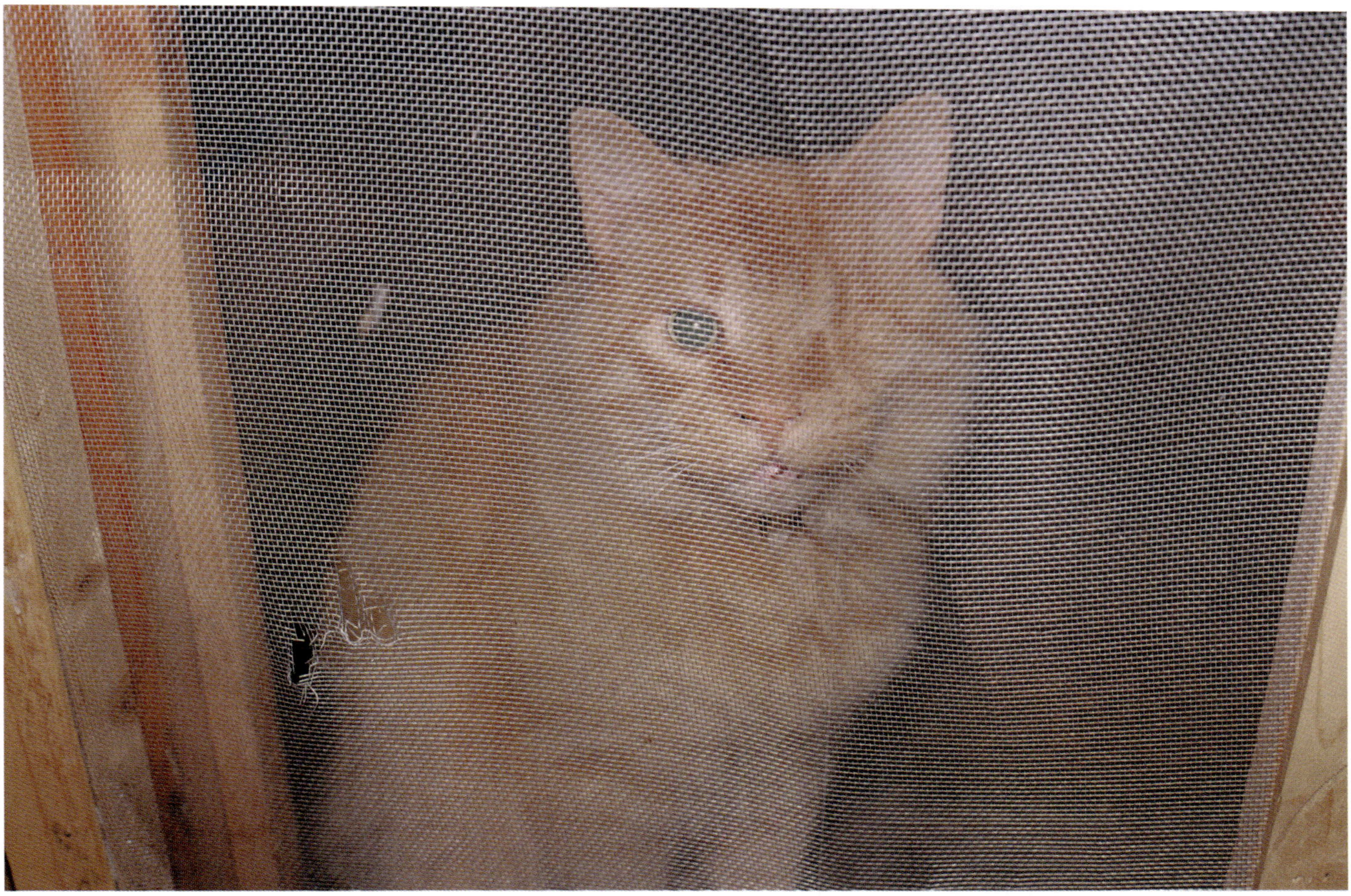

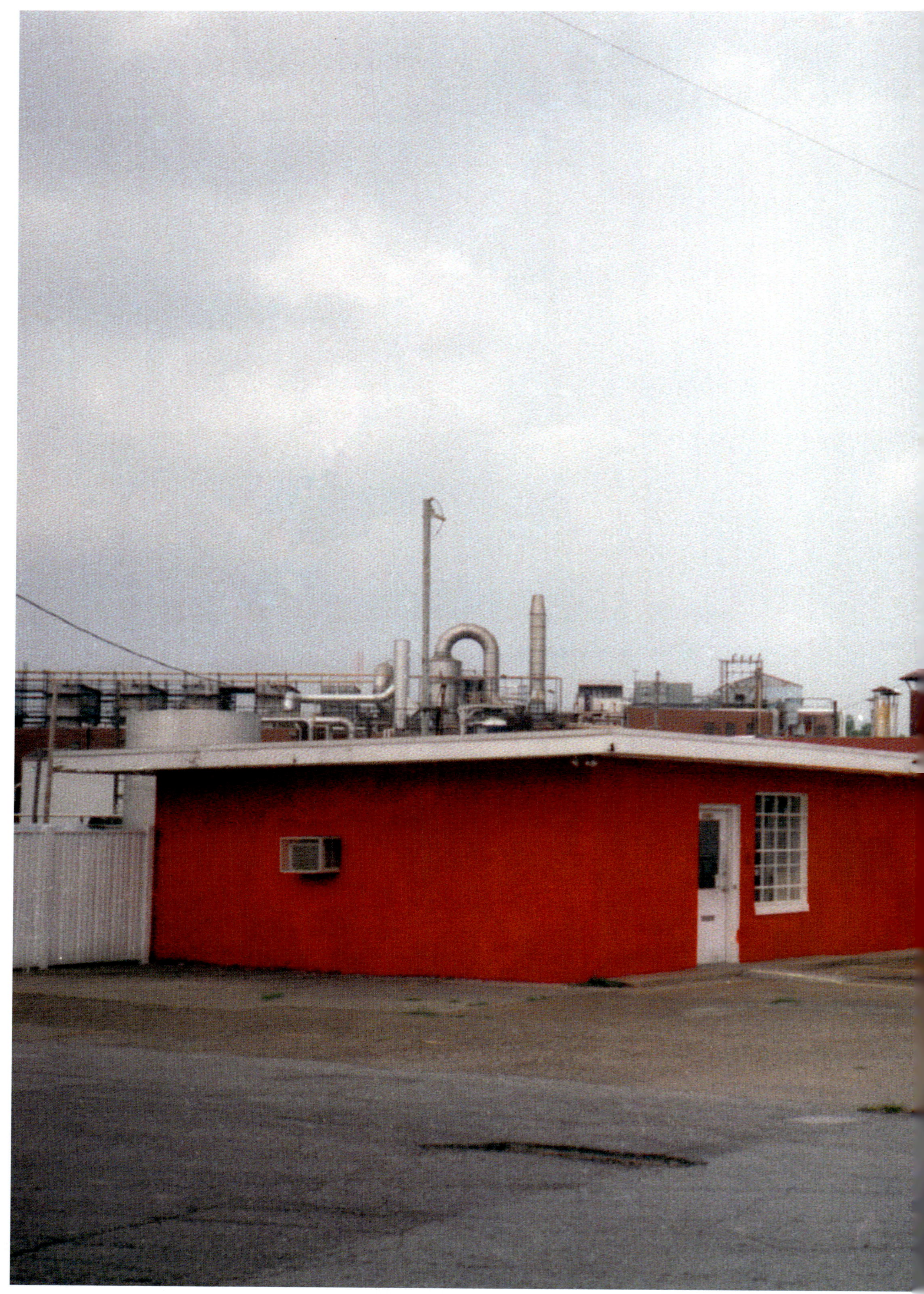

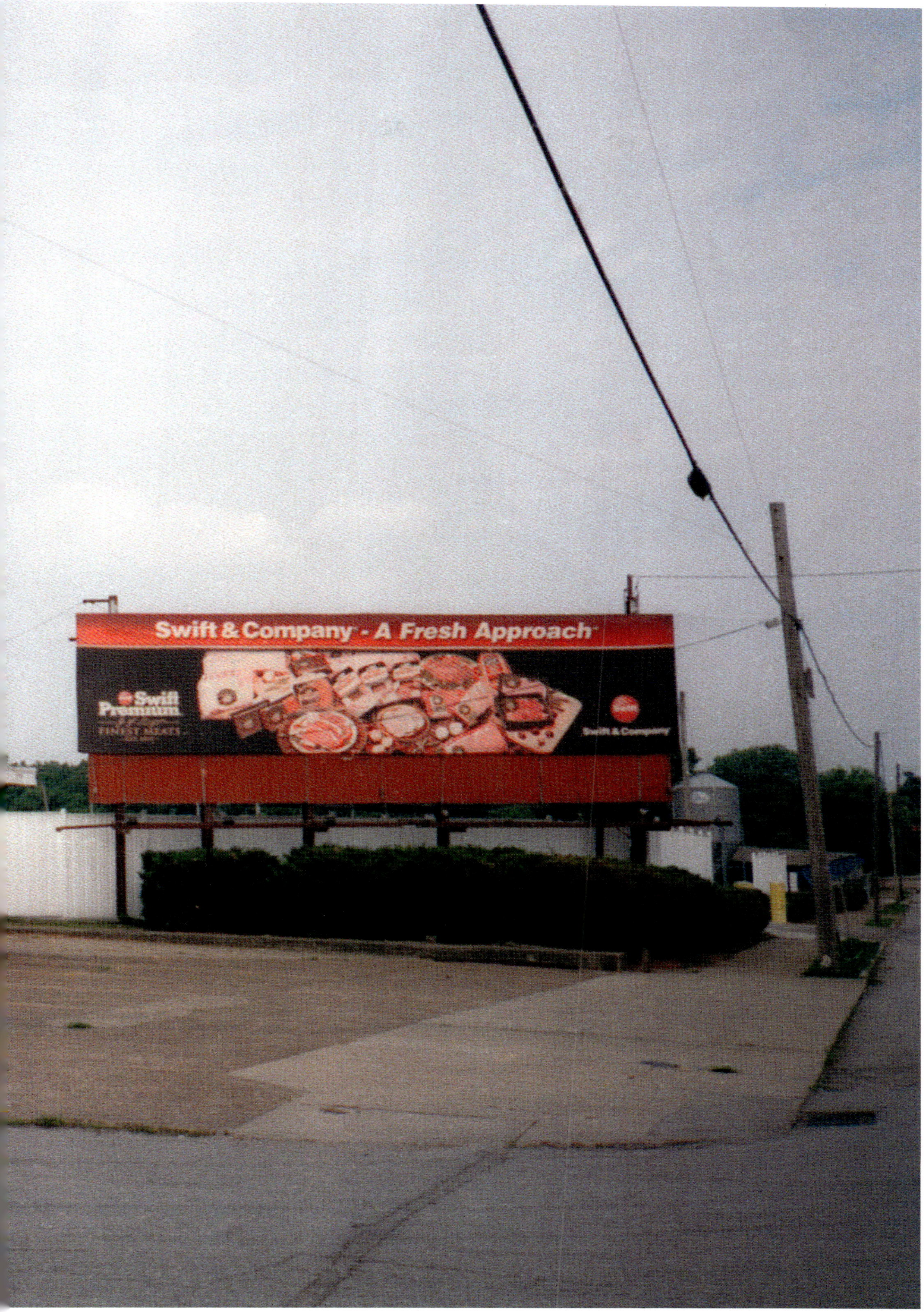

Swift & Company - A Fresh Approach
Swift Premium
FINEST MEATS
Swift & Company

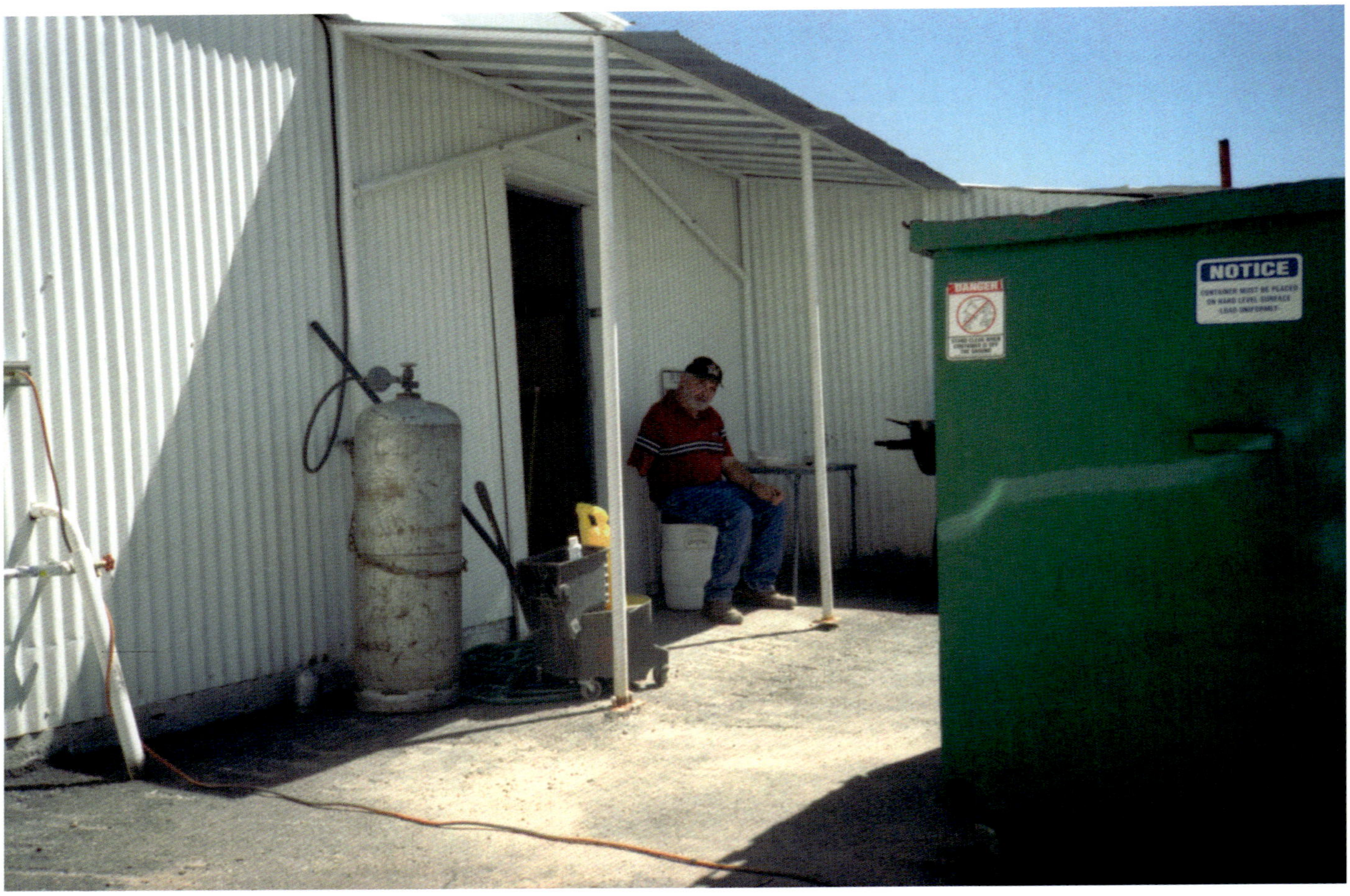
DANGER
NOTICE

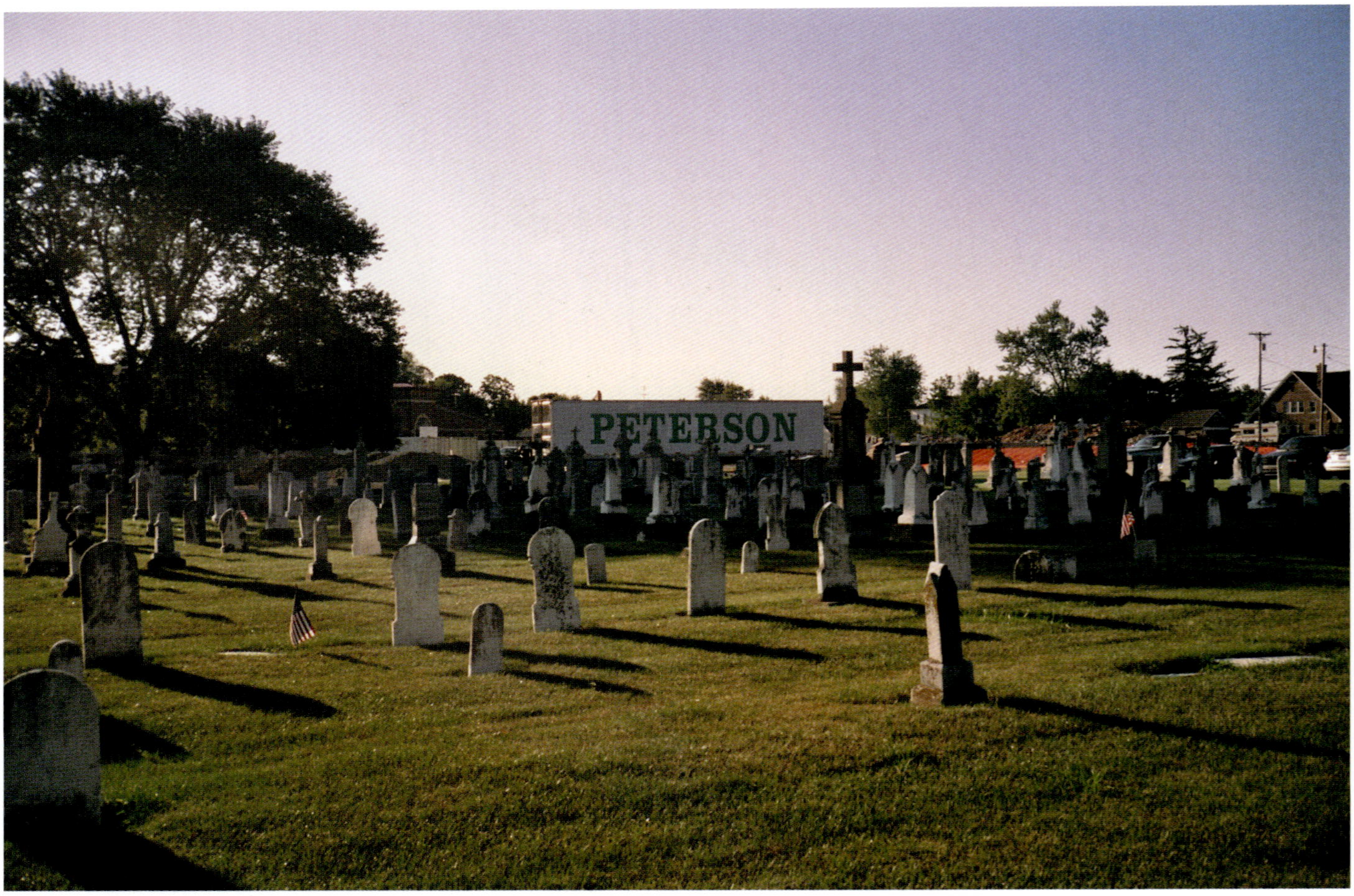
PETERSON

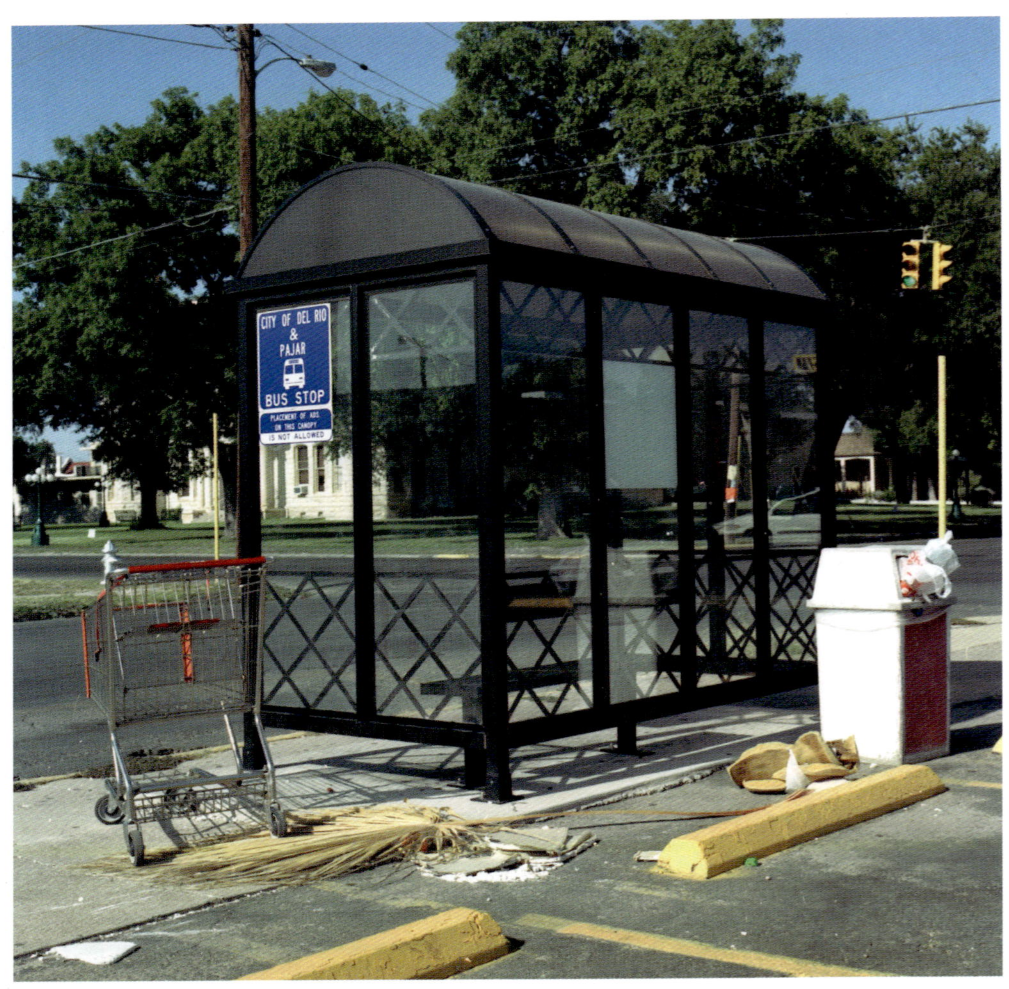
CITY OF DEL RIO
&
PAJAR
BUS STOP
PLACEMENT OF ADS
ON THIS CANOPY
IS NOT ALLOWED

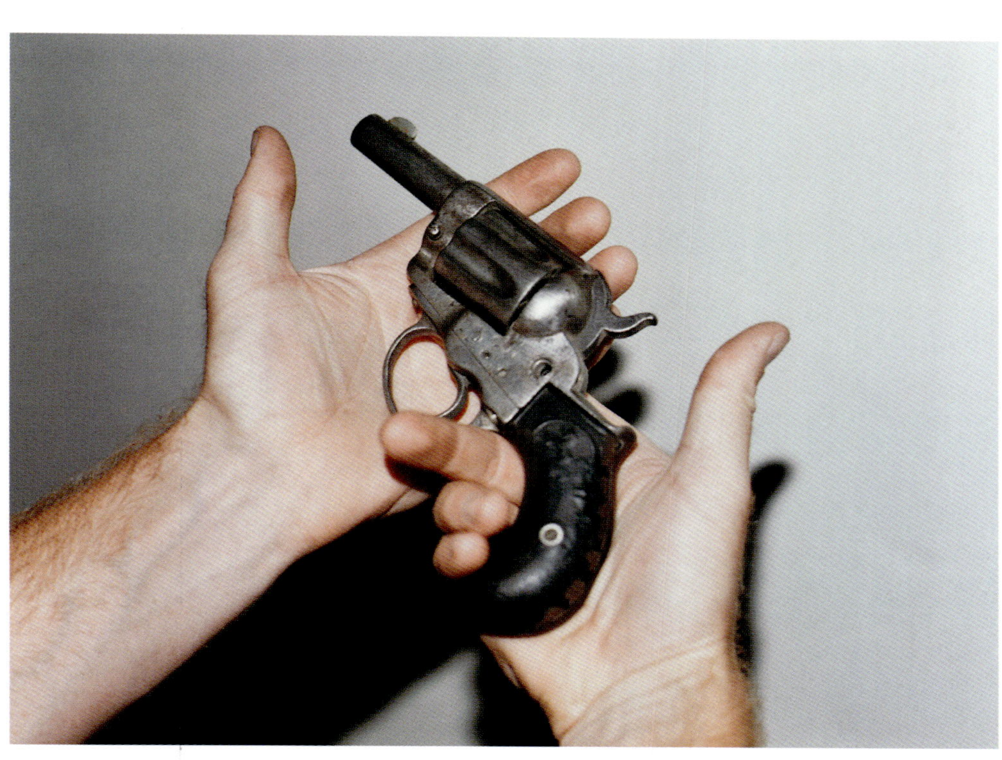

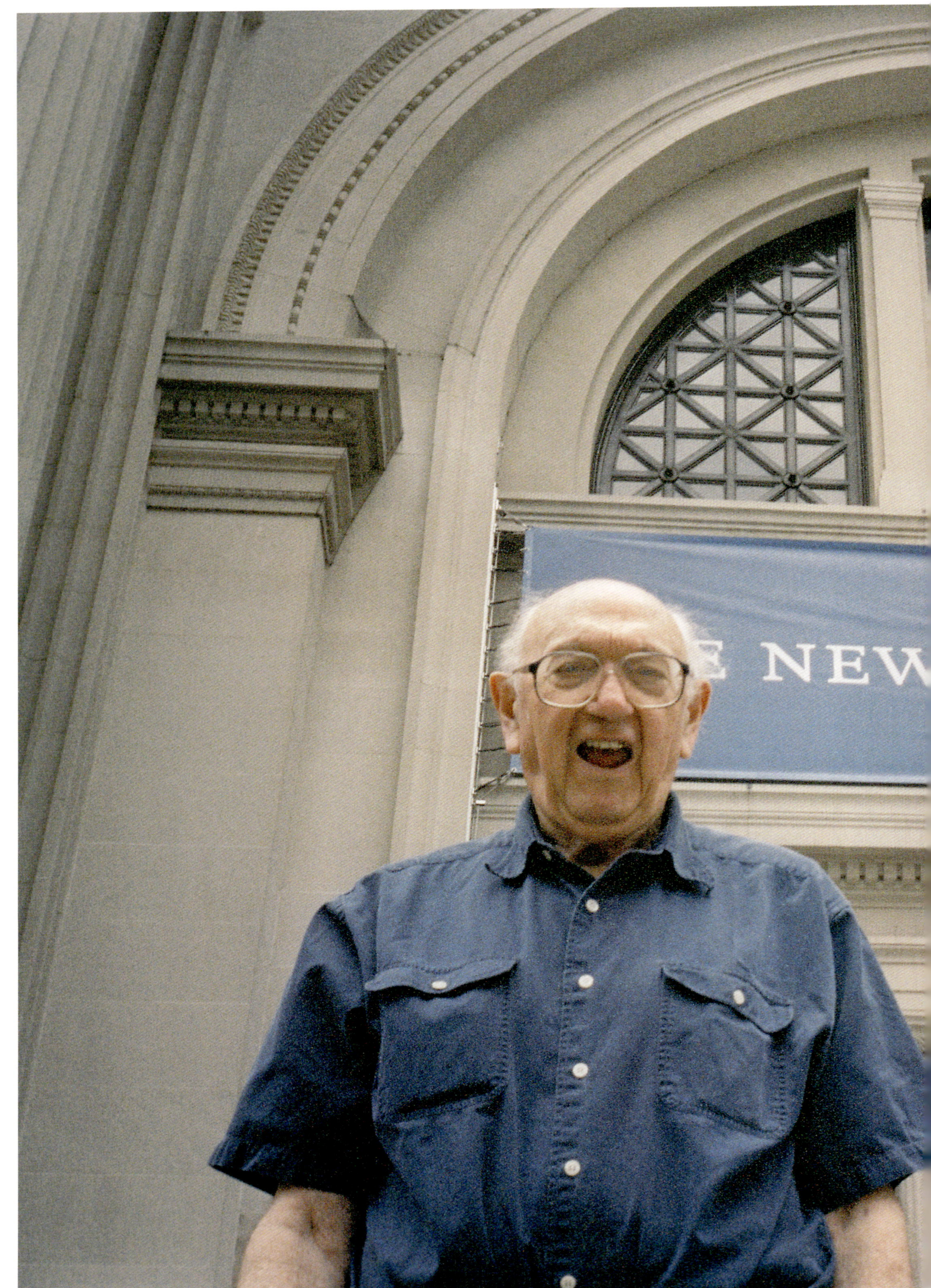
E NEW

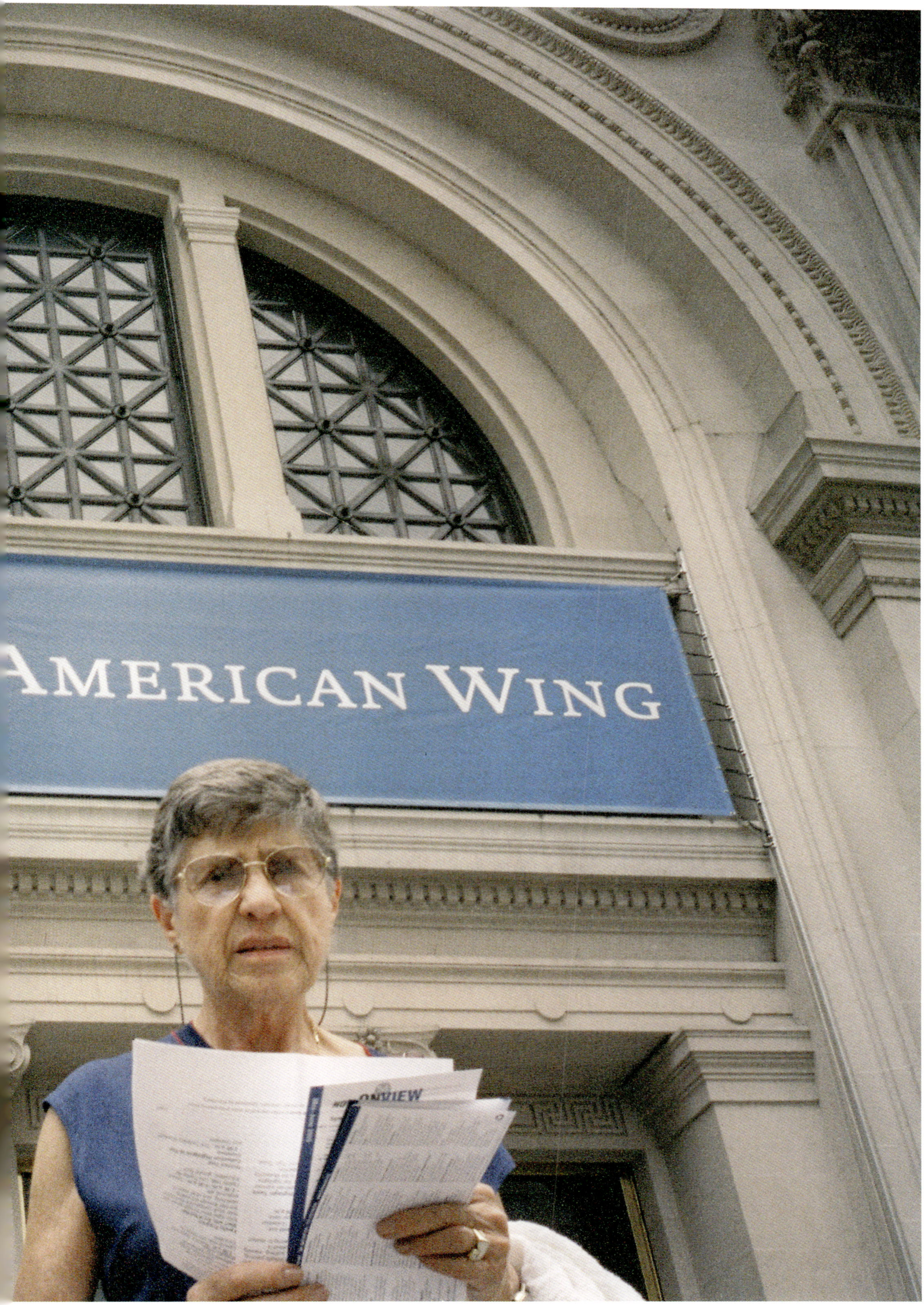

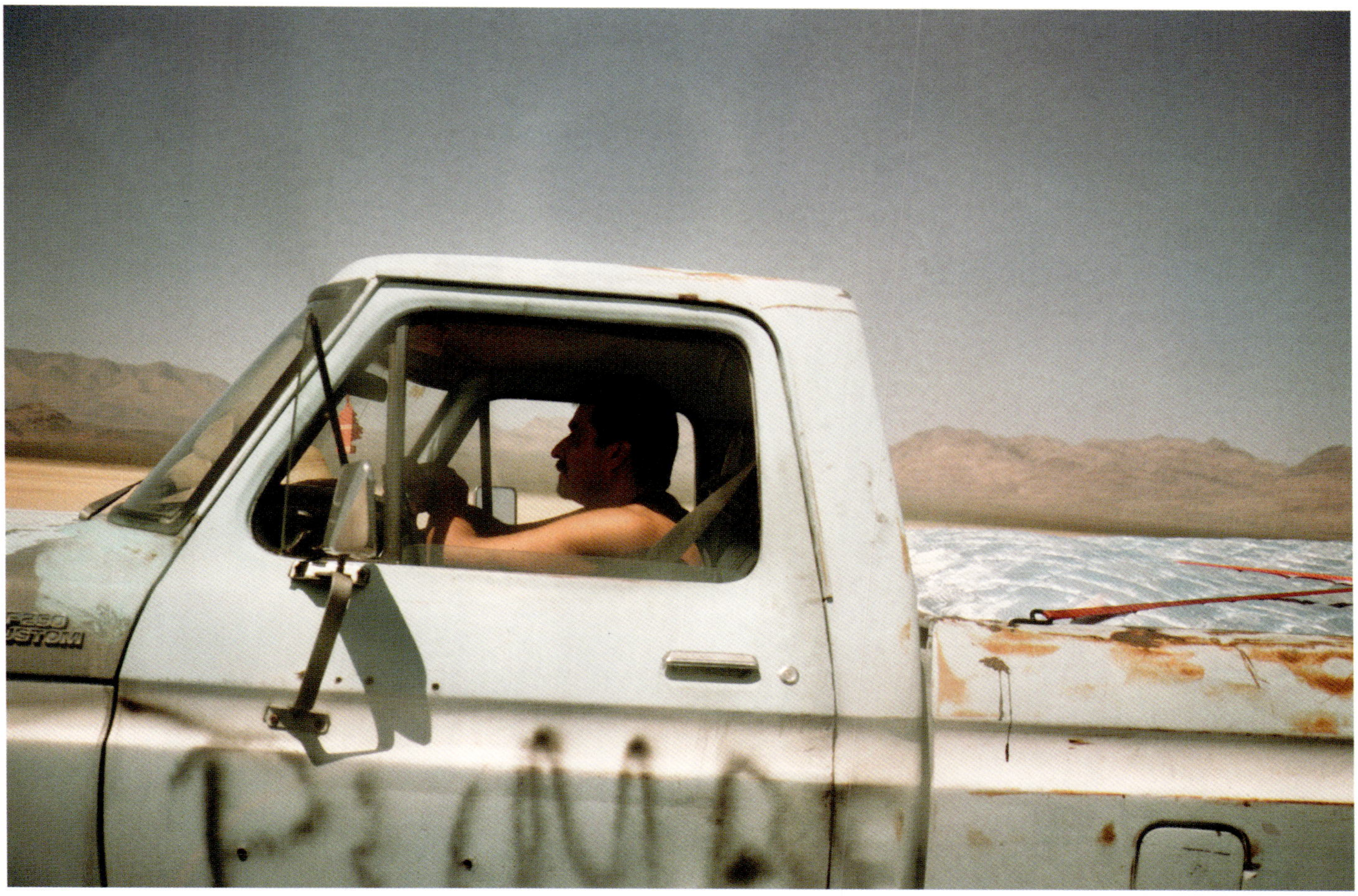

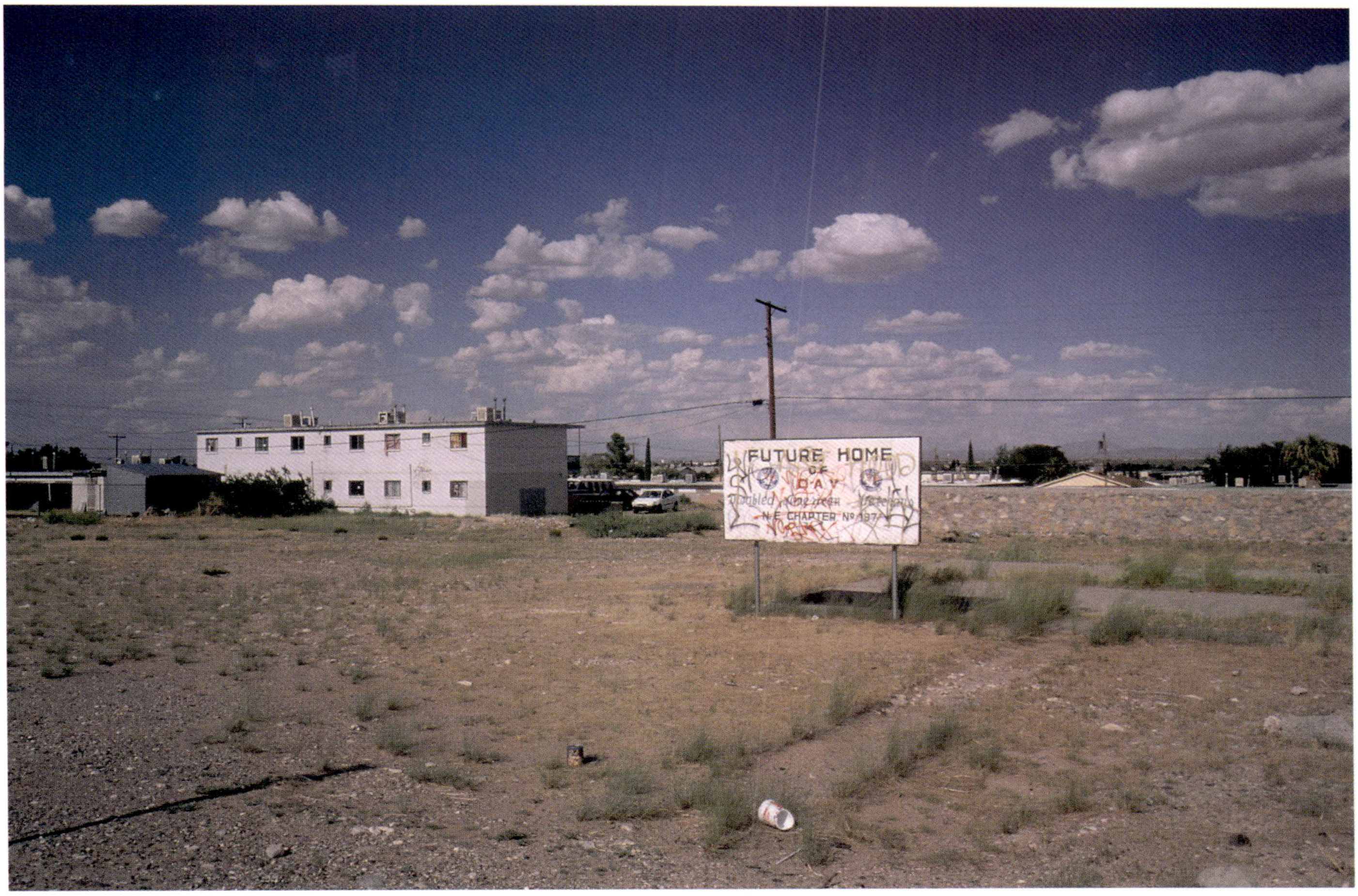

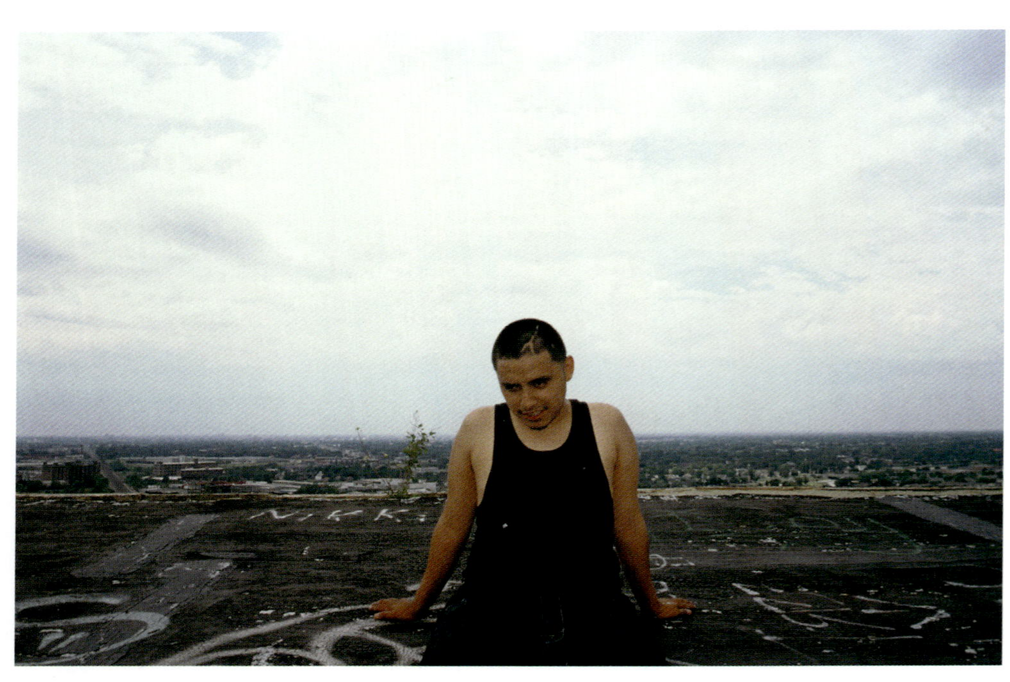

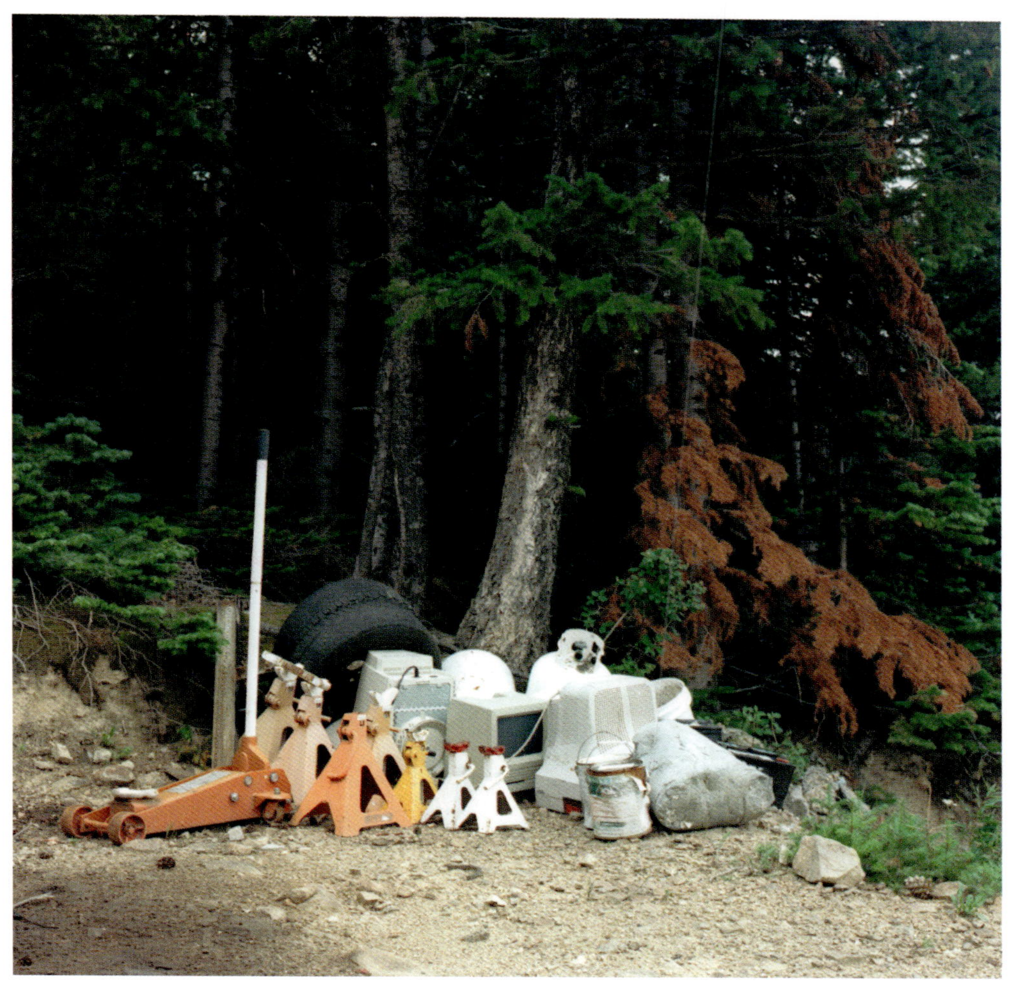

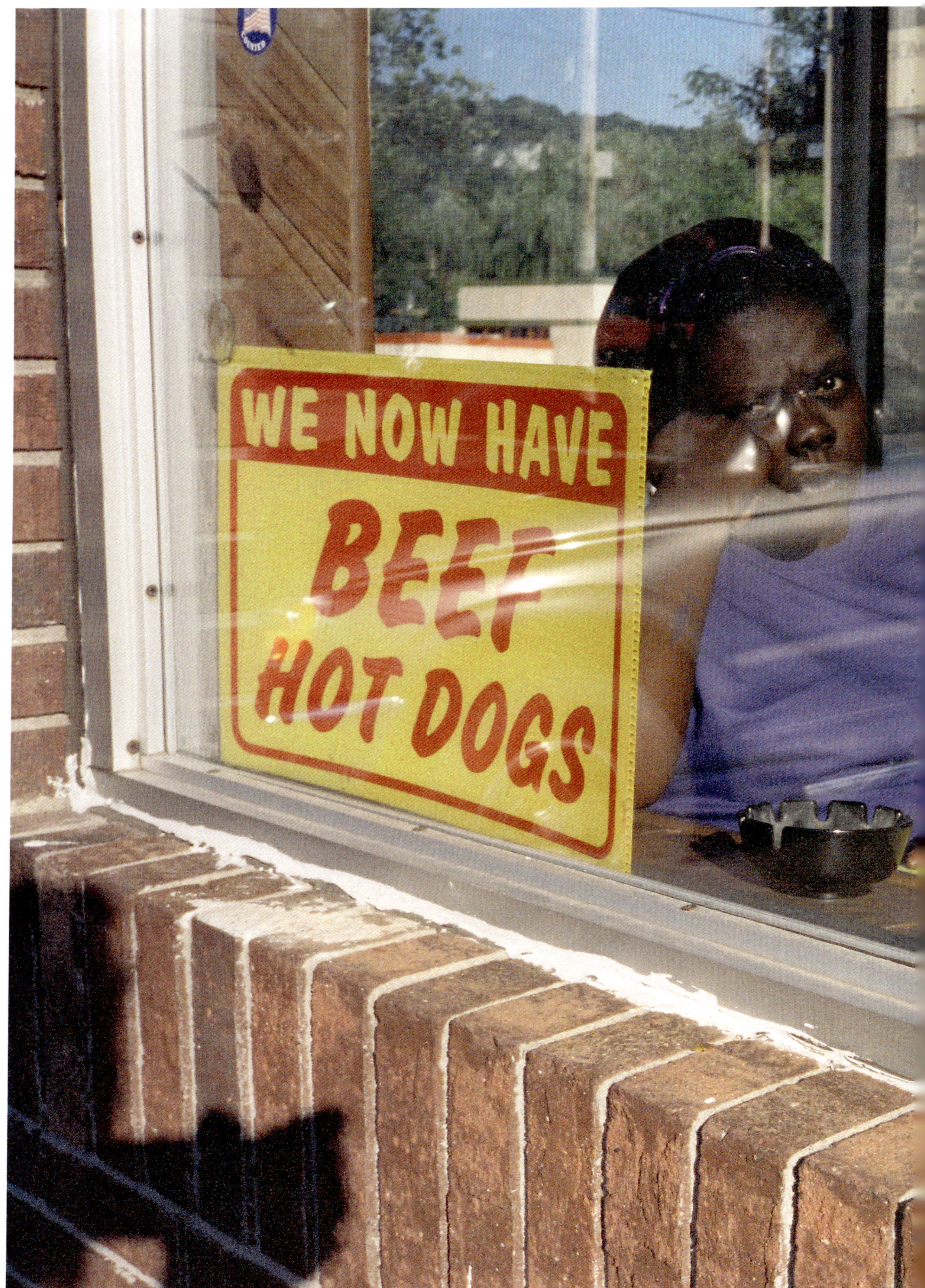
WE NOW HAVE
BEEF
HOT DOGS

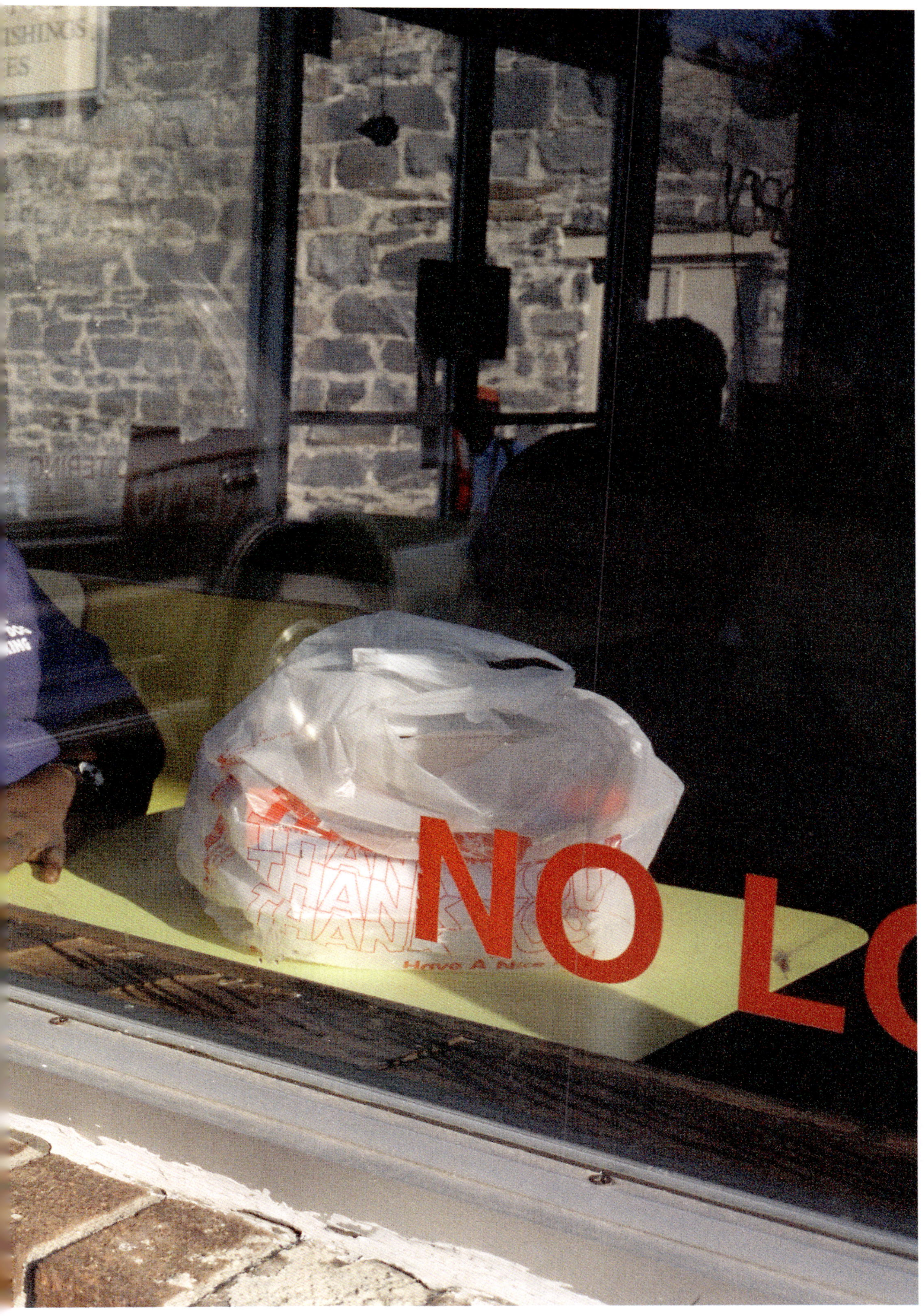
NO

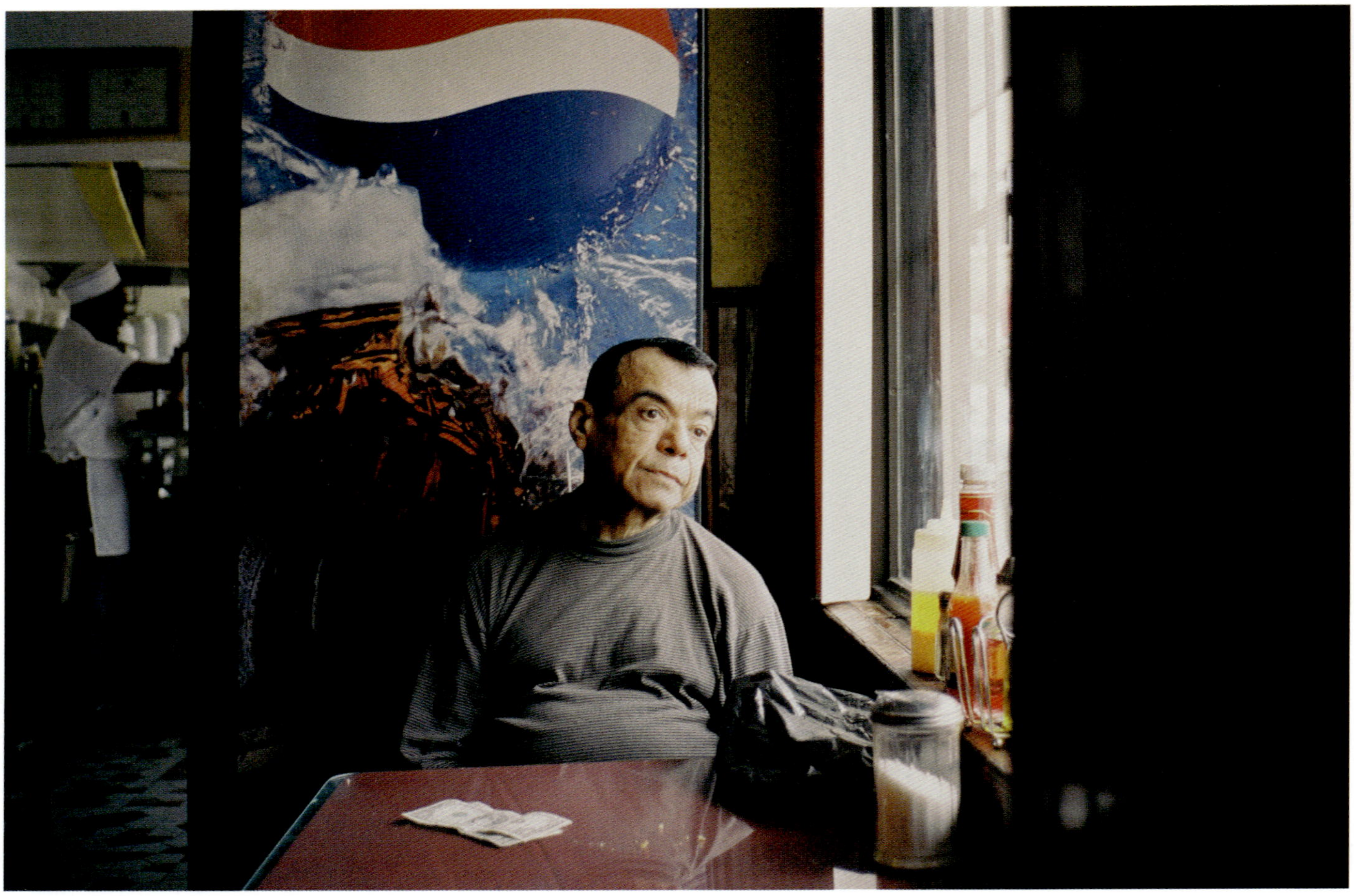

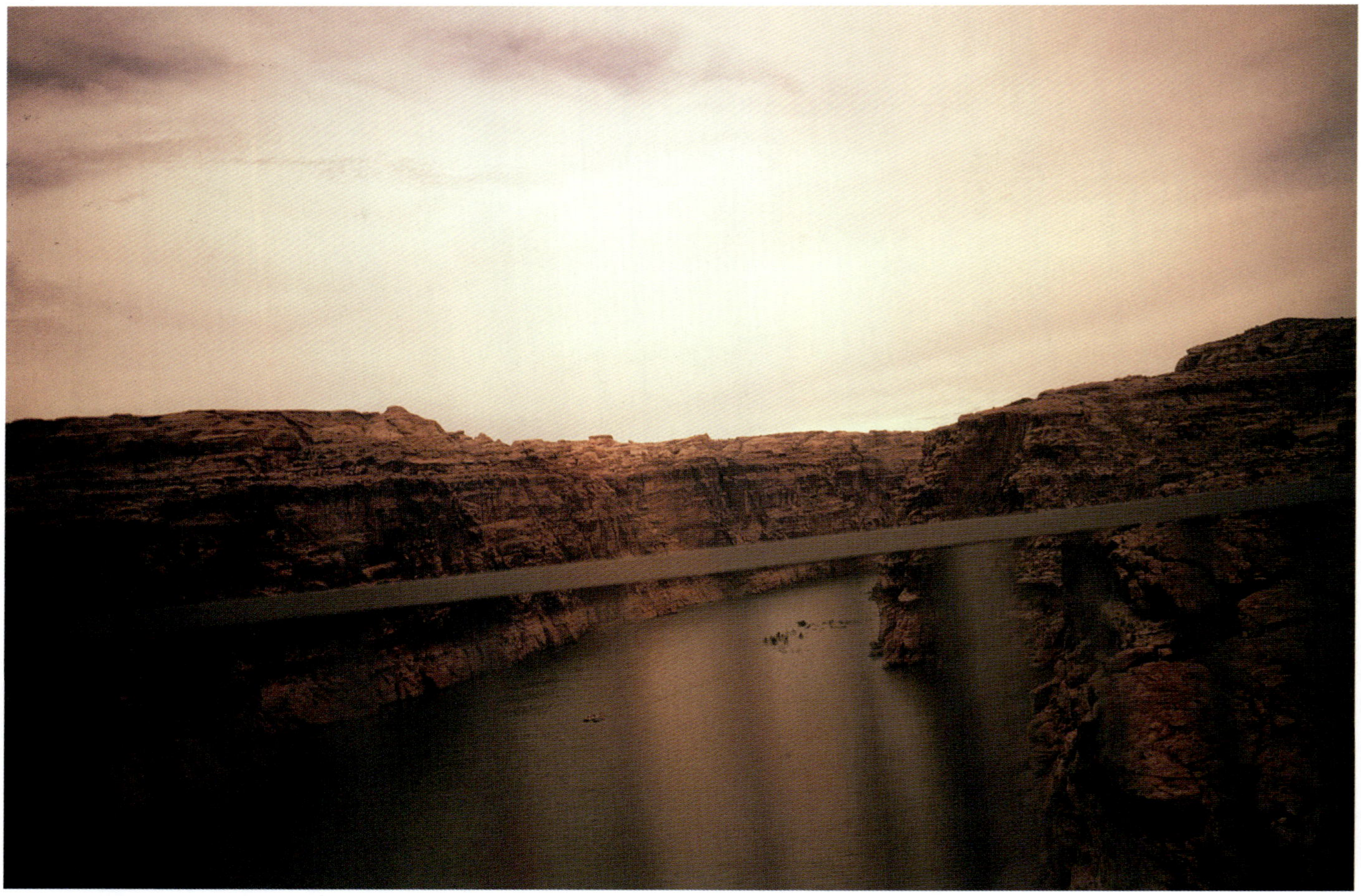

"The appearance of a human being is something that isn't self evident or something that can be taken for granted, and there's very few places in our situation where something like that can take place." – John Maus

A conversation with Benjamin Acree.

(......)

B.A.

That was the thing; everyone we met was somehow already aware of the process. Not only because of the ubiquity of cameras and images, but also because people are very aware of the concept of photographers travelling around taking pictures, and almost everyone we met already had a pose or face ready for the camera, everyone had an idea of themselves that they wanted to present. Not that people instantly thought of Stephan Shore or Robert Frank the moment we walked up, but their work is part of a larger body of work that in some ways really informs the way people think of themselves as Americans. The idea of the 'American Road Trip Photography Project' is such worn territory that it gave us access and an approach that normally wouldn't be open.

J.O.

What kind of approach?

B.A.

Well, we were interested in the way that people offered themselves to the camera, but we wanted to catch them in the process of developing their responses. Most of the people we encountered had a very clear idea of how they hoped to be seen, and they expressed this in their poses, their body language, and their facial expressions. What was vital for us was to catch this idea as it was being formed and manifested. We were interested in this grey area where the idea is present but not yet whole. And this wouldn't be possible unless everyone was already aware of our role as photographers and understood the language and symbolism that we were working with.

And also, because of this, we rarely took pictures in secret. Many times the only interaction would be a glance, a quick flash of the camera before taking the shot, to give people an idea of what we were up to. A lot of the time pictures were taken in conjunction with the subjects. Like the guy Harrison (p.56) we met who was mentally challenged, but instantly took charge of the situation, choosing where to pose, telling us where to stand, and then insisting to be tagged in the photos on Facebook. Or the woman in New Mexico (p.49) who both agreed and disagreed to have her picture taken, covering her face at the last minute, worried that her picture would be used "for pornography on the internet." People had very specific, but divergent, notions about what we were doing and what we were producing, and this gave us room to operate.

J.O.

I see how this relates to the people, but what about the pictures of landscapes and objects? How does that fit?

B.A.

The mythology involved with the growth and expansion of America is almost grafted onto the landscape, and because it has the unique distinction as a country that grew up with the advent of photography, this mythology is largely understood through images. Whether we are talking about the violence of settling the wilderness in the early days of 'The West', or of travelling through the vast expanse of open roads and rest stops and cheap motels, or the self-sufficiency and religion almost necessary for rural life; these are things that Americans understand in a visceral and very visual way. 'The Photographer' is a character in this mythology, and because we took on that role, we had access to a symbolism that people understood and offered, but also that was present in the objects and landscapes that we shot. Just as the people we photographed had a viewpoint in mind while posing, most of the objects and landscapes we were interested in also had a viewpoint that was almost built in, and with this we are able to approach the inanimate objects in much the same way as we approached the people we photographed.

J.O.

If you were looking for these ideas in places as well as people, where were some places that held your interest? Did you have a set plan?

B.A.

Initially we only had a few places in mind to visit, but the two that were most fruitful were Detroit, Michigan and Centralia, Pennsylvania. Centralia (p.62) was evacuated in 1962 because of a mine fire below the town, and the fire is still burning. The interstate had to be re-routed because the road had burst and smoke was pouring from the cracks. They think it will be burning for another hundred years. In Detroit we were able to get into the Michigan Central Station (p.2), which had been abandoned in 1988 and was slated for demolition. When it was built in 1913 it was the tallest train station in the world, and now it sits on the outskirts as a sort of sad emblem of the disasters that have taken place in the city over the years. In both instances we have places that are imbued with a large degree of symbolism, but both coming undone and in a state of flux.

J.O.

It is good to know some the background for those pictures. Are there any others that you feel need some context?

B.A.

Absolutely. That pistol (p.37), that had been owned by Bill the Kid. That should probably be mentioned. This dog (p.22) was almost killed by a rattlesnake, and then shortly after this picture was taken it was hit by a car and died. The man with the eagle tattoo (p.18) also died, but of lung cancer. The boy with a scar on his head (p.42), this was in Detroit on the roof of the Train Depot. He was showing us the scars from where he was ambushed and beaten with a bat.

J.O.

You met him on the roof?

B.A.

We met him and his friends in the basement, and we were terrified, but they gave us a tour of the building and took us up to the roof, where they described the city. He pointed out day-to-day things, houses, bars, schools, as well as more important landmarks; the hospital where his daughter was born, neighborhoods to avoid, places burned during Halloween arsons. They told us that they broke into the Train Depot twice a day. They had rigged a series of lights around the tip of the building and had to come in to turn them on nightly, and then return in the morning to shut them off. It was a tag, a beacon that could be seen everywhere in the city. They said no matter where they were, they could point up to the building and say "That's us."

As we looked down back at the city, I imagined them as they had just described themselves, situated directly between their symbol and the neighborhoods they had come from, looking back up to their lights strung across the roof. They appeared vividly in their descriptions, and it is clear that appearing in this way isn't something self-evident or something that can be taken for granted. This is the view that we aimed for with these photographs, and if through this book we can even partially approximate this experience, I think we will have achieved something with meaning, something worthwhile.

(......)

Perth, September 12th 2011

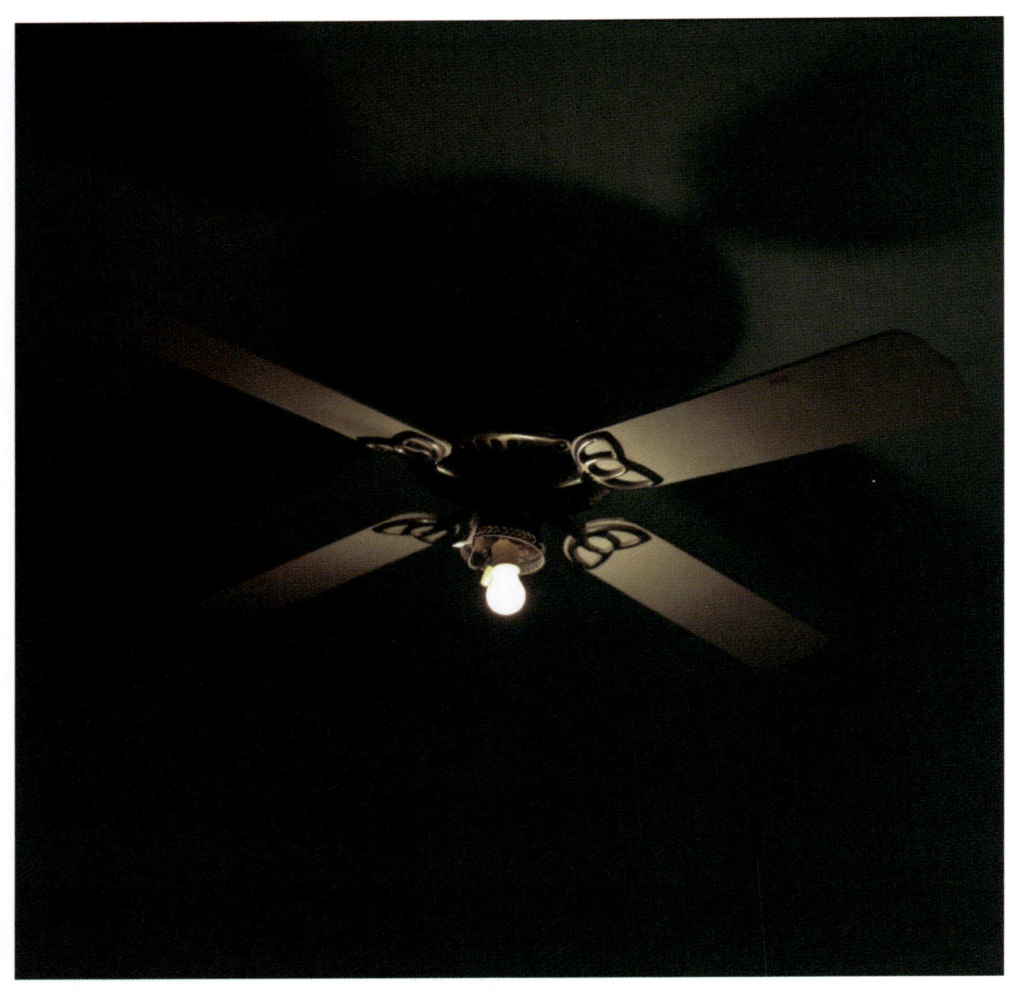

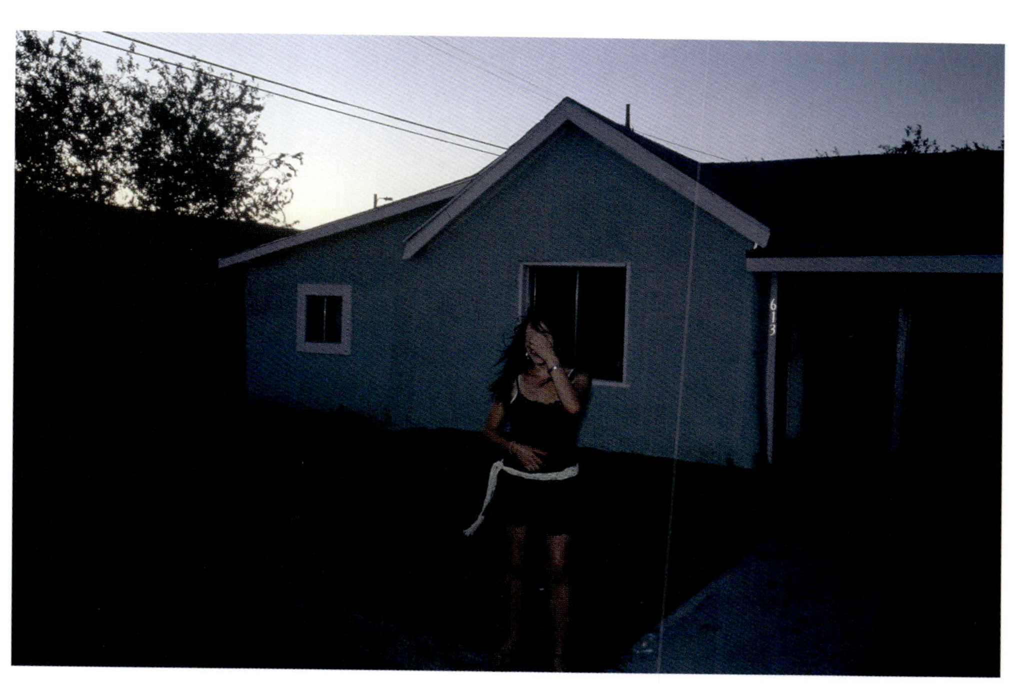

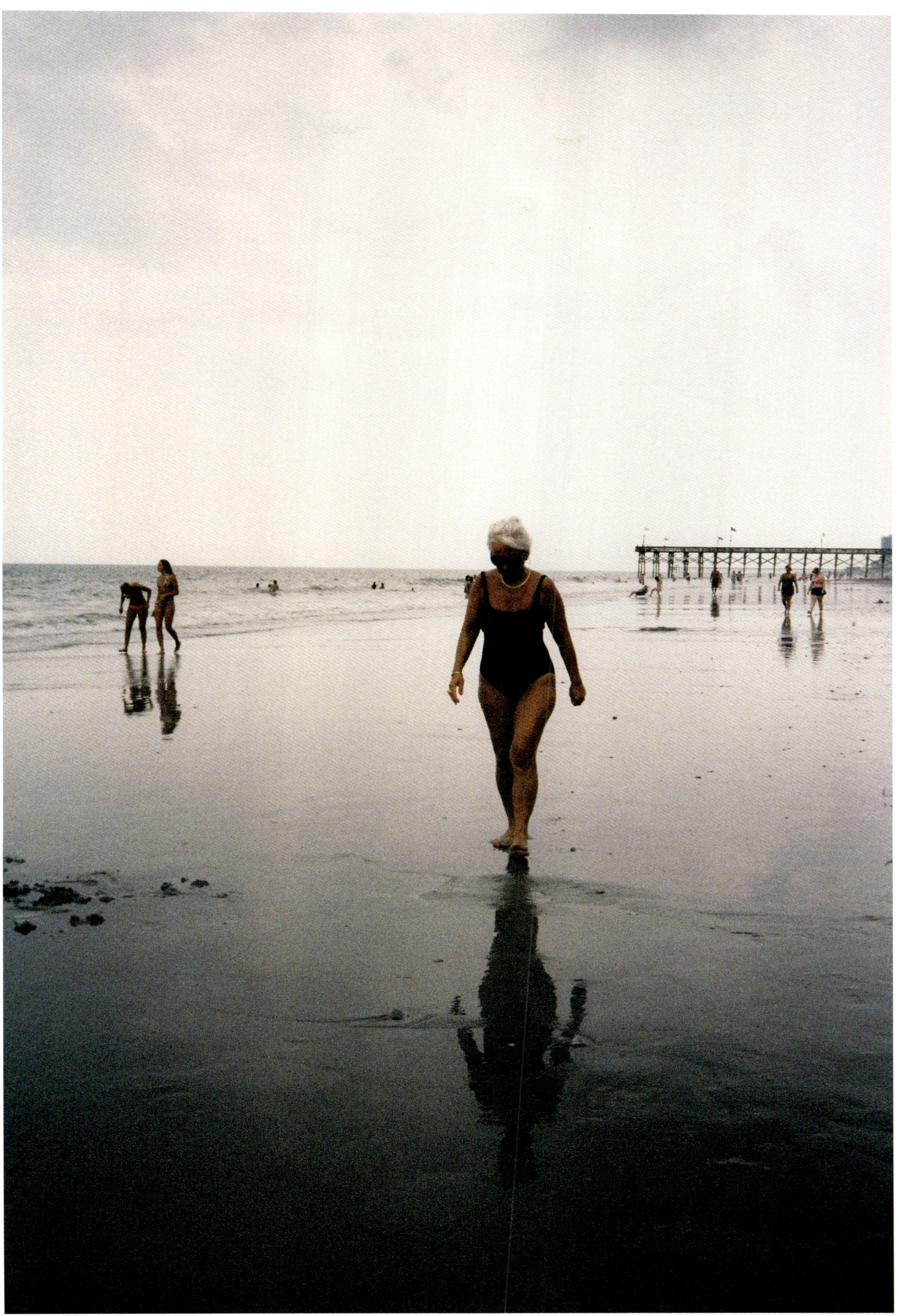

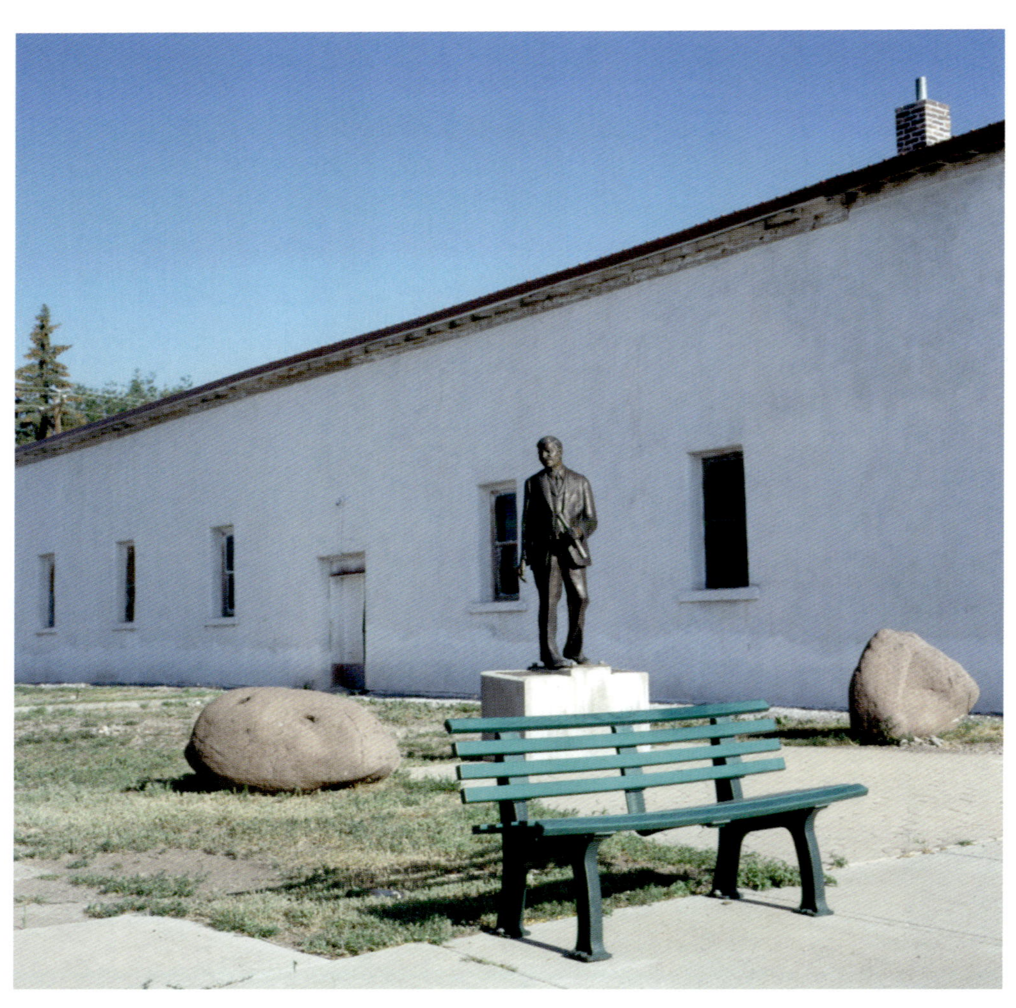

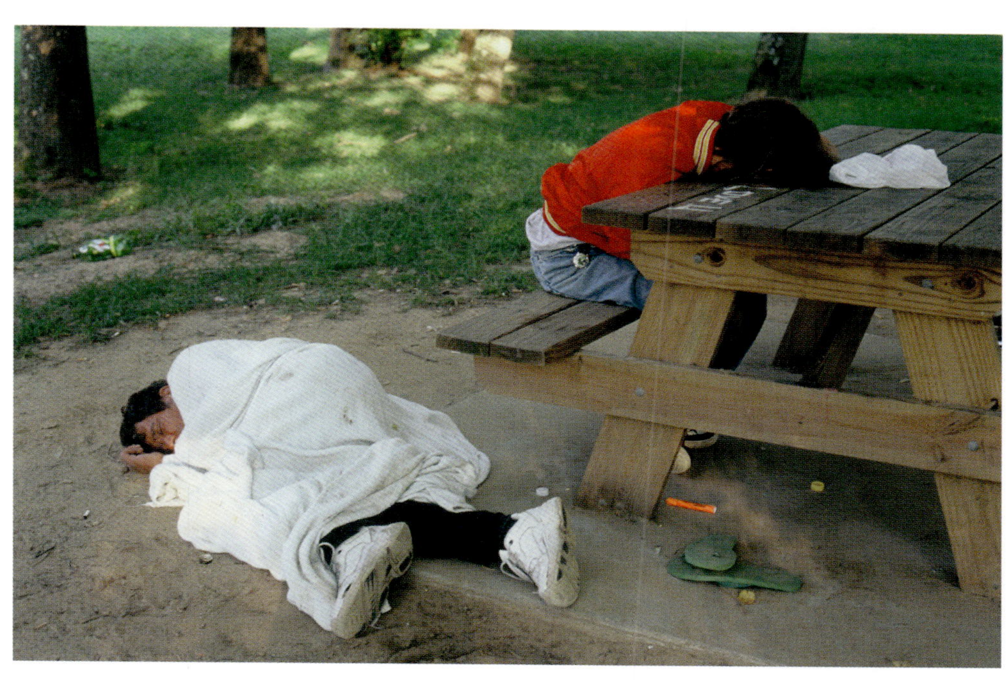

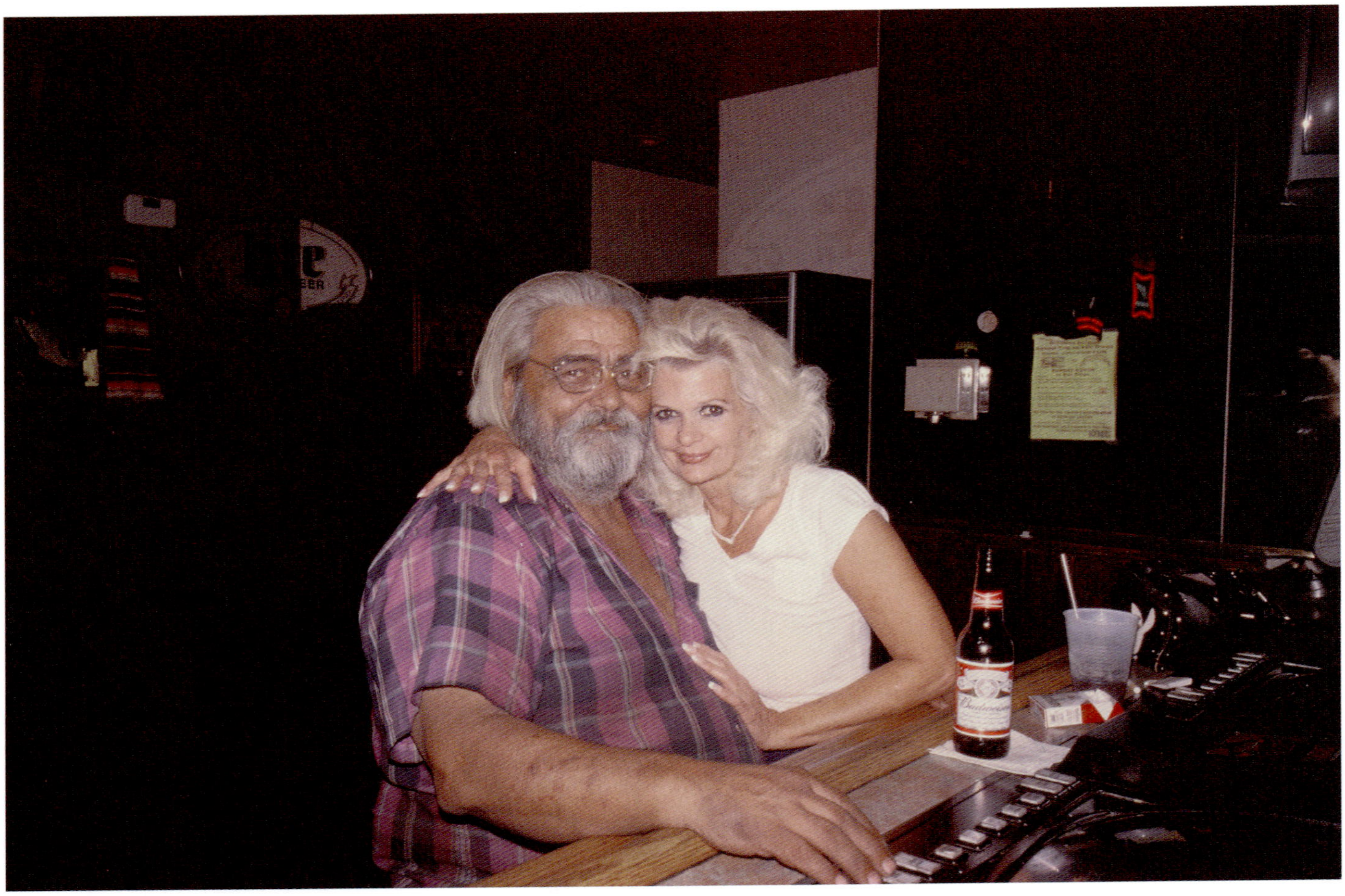

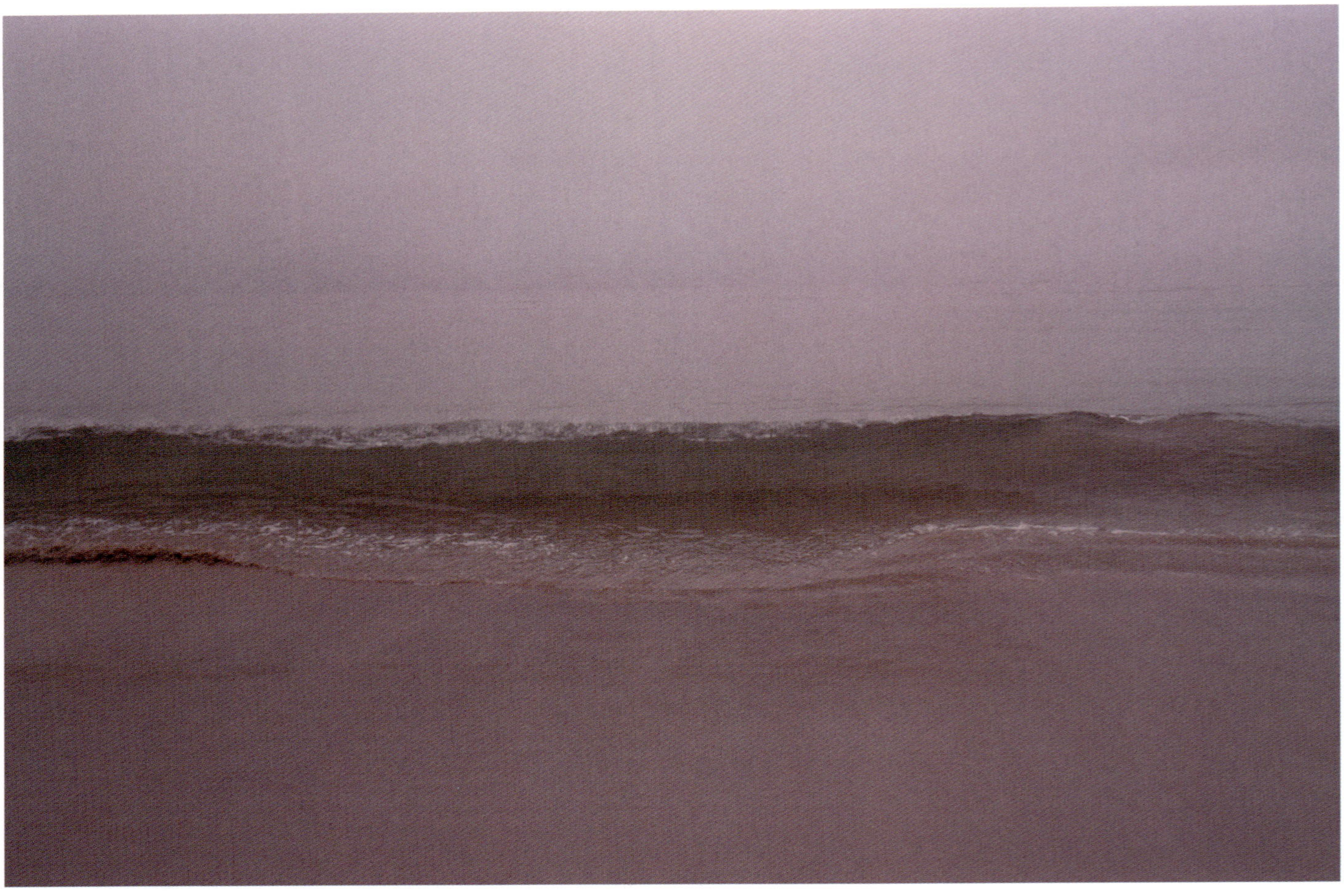

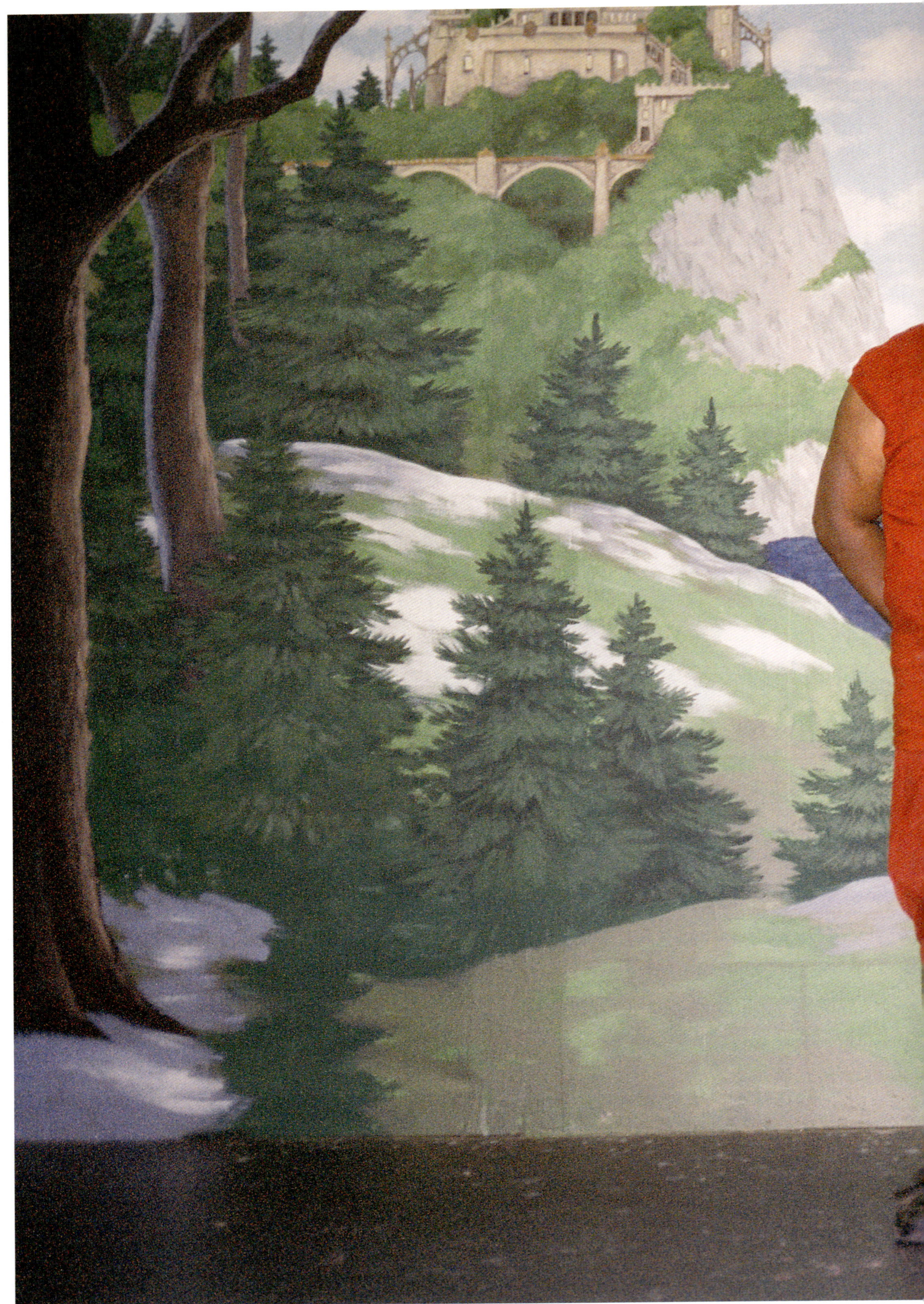

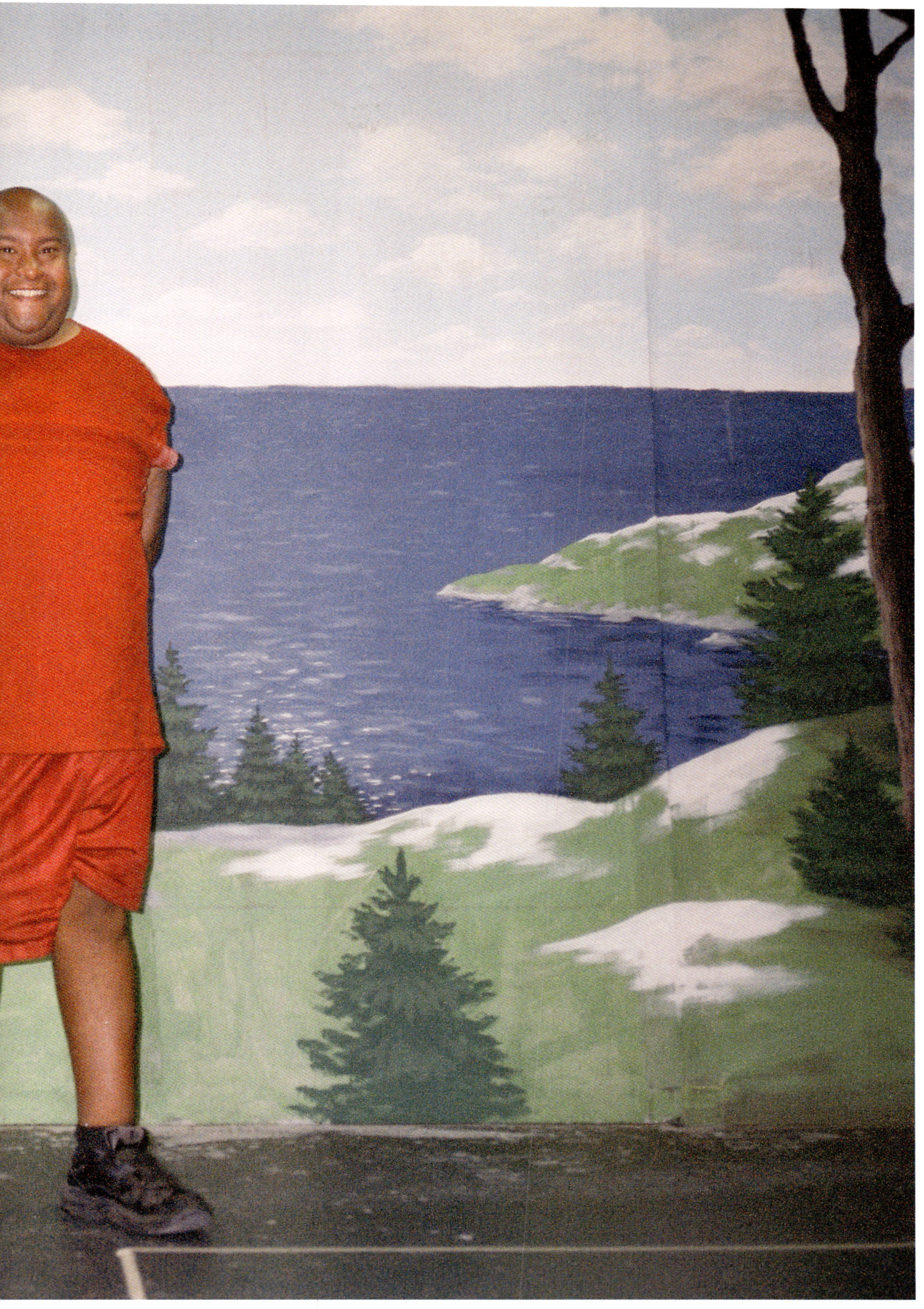

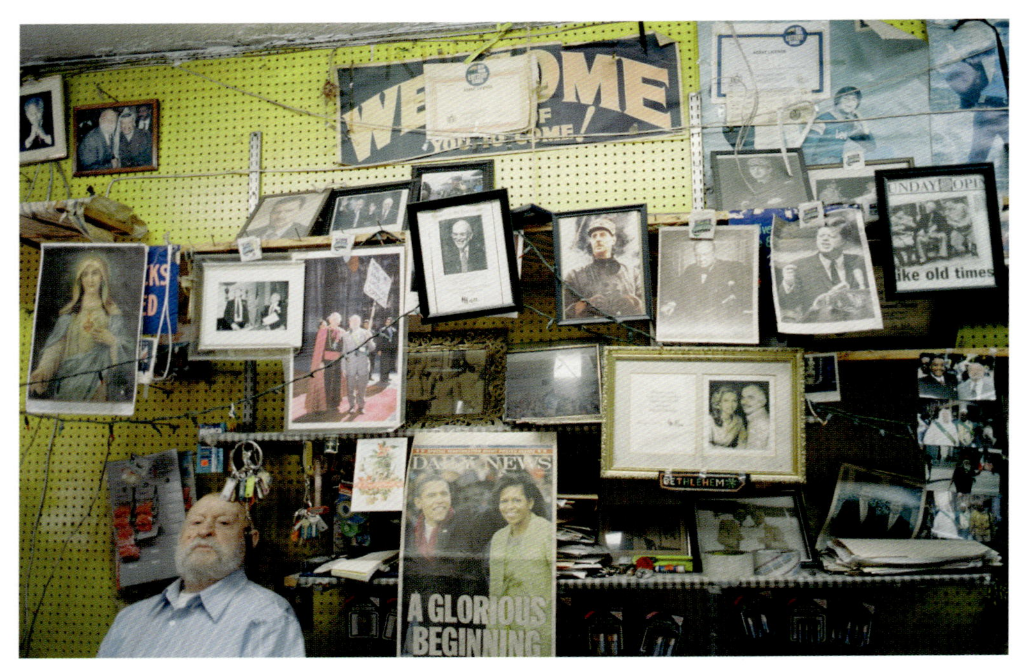

WELCOME
like old times
BETHLEHEM
A GLORIOUS BEGINNING

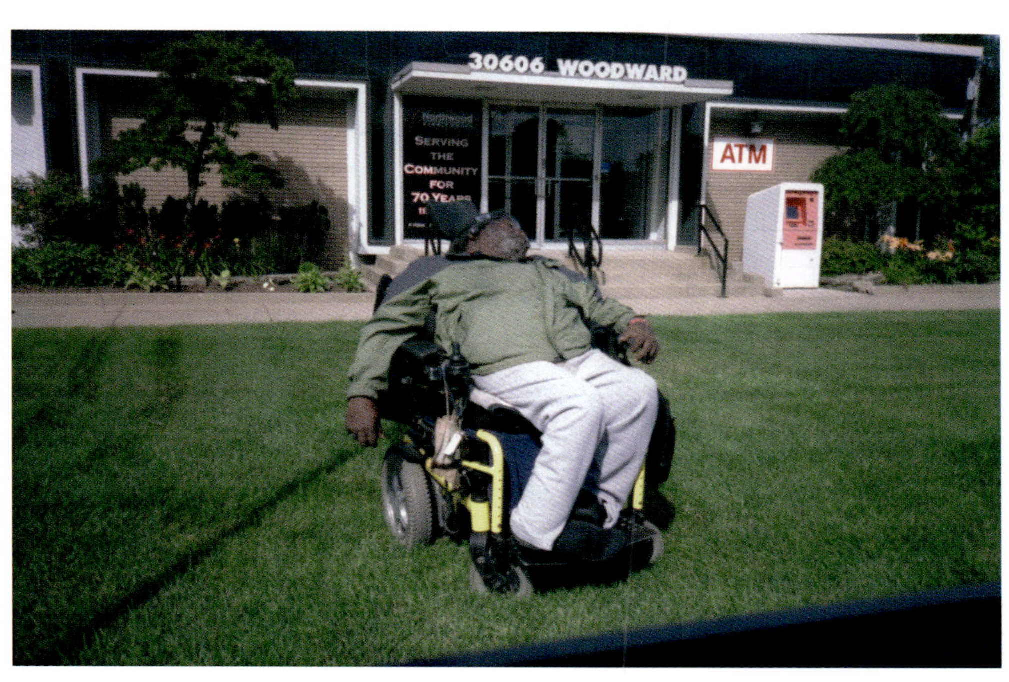
30606 WOODWARD
SERVING
THE
COMMUNITY
FOR
70 YEARS
ATM

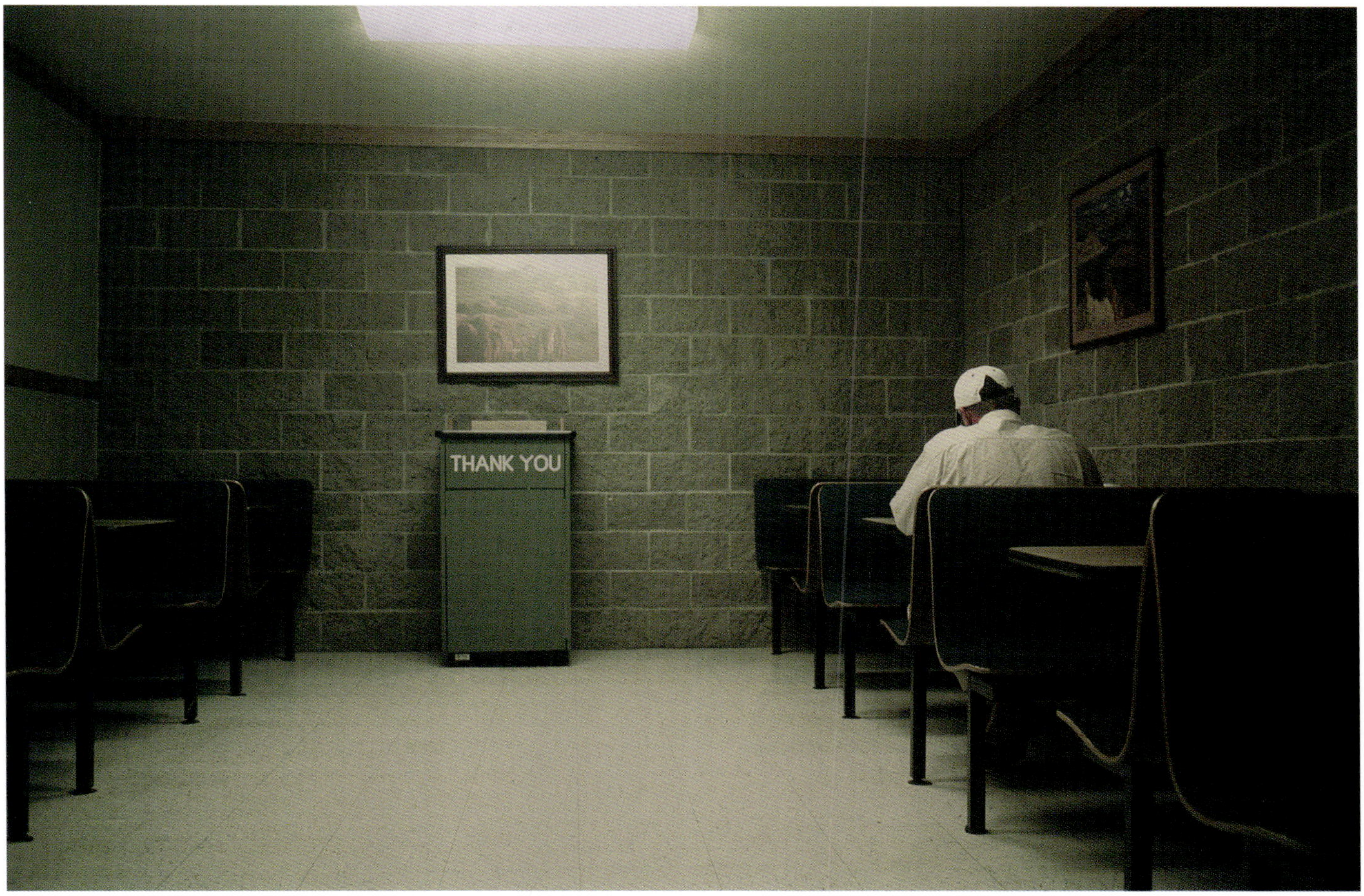

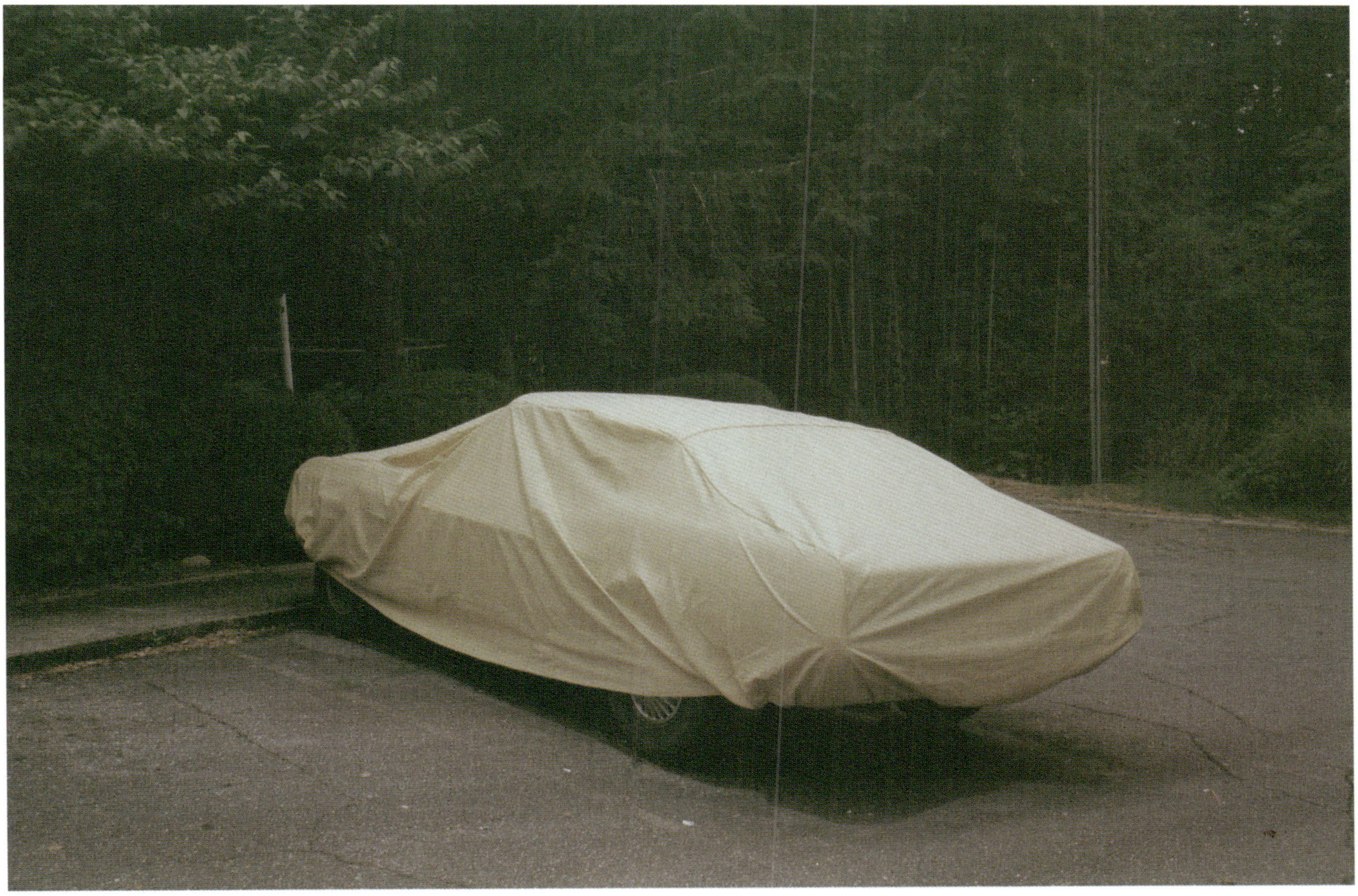

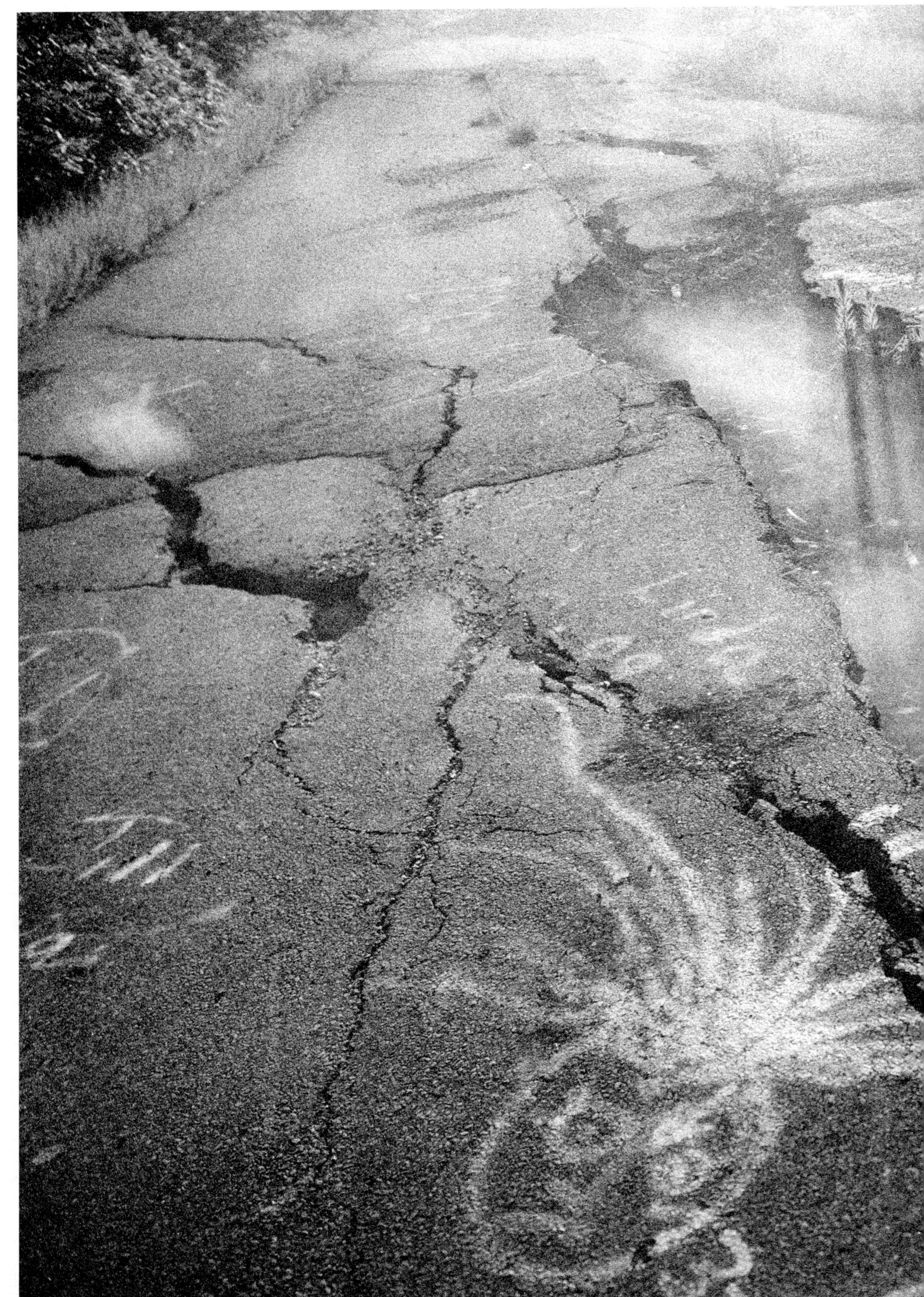